POLAR BEAR
EXPRESS

polarbear
e x p r e s s

Forestry along the
Polar Bear Express

LAKE
ABITIBI

MODEL FOREST
NETWORK

RÉSEAU DE
FORÊTS MODÈLES

You are about to embark on a wonderful journey through the Boreal Forest – hundreds of thousands of square kilometres of trees, wetlands, significant waterways, and fascinating natural and human history... some within the Great Northern Claybelt, the remnants of what was once an immense post-glacial lake called Barlow-Ojibway. This is your opportunity to both enjoy and learn about the area's interesting forest history as well as boreal ecosystems and how they function, and how they are managed sustainably...

1 Cochrane Area Forestry (Mile 0)

Logging in the local area began in earnest with the completion of the Ontario Northland Railway (ONR) from New Liskeard to Cochrane in 1908, and the National Trans-Continental Railway (later the CNR) from Quebec City to western Canada; harvested timber was primarily used for railway ties and to build bridges. The area became accessible and well promoted by the government of the time, with its vast forests and potential for successful settlement and farming. The town of Cochrane itself was founded in 1908 and incorporated in 1910; its name selected to honour Frank Cochrane, then Ontario Minister of Lands, Forests and Mines. As the town grew, several sawmills were established that provided lumber for construction. In 1912, the company now known as Abitibi-Consolidated Company of Canada began harvesting north of Cochrane, building a pulp and paper mill in Iroquois Falls. The mill began operating in 1914, initially using wood produced from land being cleared for farming.

Present forestry operations in the area are sustainable and have increased gradually during the past century. The area annually harvested averages about 12,000 hectares. Approximately 6,000 hectares are artificially regenerated (planted or aerial seeded) and the remainder is allowed to naturally regenerate. The major forest industries include a pulp and paper mill owned by Tembec Industries Inc., located to the west of Cochrane at Smooth Rock Falls. A second pulp and paper mill is operated by Abitibi-Consolidated Company of Canada, located in Iroquois Falls, south  of Cochrane. In the town itself, Tembec Industries Inc. owns a sawmill and Norbord Industries Inc. operates a plywood plant.

2 Succession (Mile 1 – 10)

As we leave Cochrane, the rail line heads north through active and abandoned farms that were cleared during the settlement of the area in the 1920's and 1930's. Some of these farms were abandoned many years later for a variety of reasons. You may notice that various shrubs and trees have moved into the cleared fields through a process called  'succession' *(the natural change in vegetation from simple grasses and herbs toward more complex vegetation, such as trees)*. The rate of change becomes more gradual with time until there appears to be no change. This stage of succession is called the 'climax community'.

As the vegetation changes, so do the wildlife habitat characteristics and ultimately the animals that inhabit the area. During early stages, birds such as Nashville, Tennessee, and Chestnut-sided Warblers are present. As successional stages progress, these warblers move out and the Black-throated Green, Blackburnian Warblers, and Hermit Thrushes take up residence. Forests and animals form complex communities that are constantly changing. At any time, a new disturbance may interrupt the sequence of successional change and start the process again. Fire, harvesting, and land clearing are examples of such disturbances. As you journey northward, most of the vegetation you will see are examples of a climax community.

3 The Abitibi River (Mile 11.4)

Historically, long before many roads were built and waterways were our only highways, the Abitibi River was effectively used to transport logs. Areas located south of the town of Iroquois Falls were harvested during winter months and  the logs piled on the frozen rivers and lakes. In the spring and summer, after the ice had melted, the logs were floated down the Abitibi River to the pulp and paper mill located in Iroquois Falls. The use of trucks to transport logs gradually increased last century until the local use of river transportation was discontinued in the mid-1970's. The brown colour of the river results from naturally occurring sediments and is common to the Great Claybelt.

4 Mixedwood Stands (Mile 15, 16.1, 20)

On both sides of the rail line you will notice what foresters call mixedwood stands *(a stand generally has the same age and mix of tree species growing in a continuous area)*. These particular mixedwood stands contain poplar, white birch, balsam fir, and spruce and they originated around 1920 to 1930. The most common and the tallest tree found in these stands is poplar, which is a deciduous species, meaning it loses its leaves every autumn. Poplar is used in the manufacture of various wood products including veneer, paper, and oriented strand board (OSB). It is used locally by Norbord Industries Inc. in plywood production.

You will also notice numerous small fires that have occurred along the tracks in recent years. These fires are caused by the railroad itself (sparks from metal wheel on metal track) but are kept in check through the efforts of the Ontario Ministry of Natural Resources and the Ontario Northland Railway.

The second most abundant tree in these stands is balsam fir, which is a coniferous species, meaning it does not lose its foliage (needles) in the fall. From a distance, balsam fir looks like a spruce tree, but it has softer needles and smoother bark. It is the medium-sized tree you see growing beneath the poplars throughout the stand. Balsam fir grows best in cold moist soils and regenerates through seed released from cones. It can grow in both shade or full sunlight, reaches maturity (full development) between 60 and 80 years of age, attains an average height of 15 to 20 metres (49 to 65 feet), and a diameter of 20 to 25 centimetres (8 to 10 inches). Balsam fir is used by local mills for lumber and paper production. With respect to wildlife, balsam fir is also important as winter browse (food) for moose. Juicy leaves and new twigs from shrubs, young poplar and white birch trees are in short supply during winter, and balsam fir help to supply the nourishment that moose require to survive. In addition, areas that contain greater than 50 per cent balsam fir are the favourite habitat of the beautiful Magnolia Warbler.

White birch is the other species you see mixed in with the poplar and balsam fir. It can be identified by its white papery bark. It is a deciduous tree which requires full sunlight to regenerate and grow. Reaching maturity between 60 to 75 years of age, white birch is a short-lived specie, with few living longer than 140 years. White birch attains an average height of 20 to 25 metres (65 to 82 feet) and an average diameter of 25 to 30 centimetres (10 to 12 inches). Most white birch regeneration occurs from new branches which sprout from roots and stumps once the tree is cut or killed by fire, insects, or disease. White birch was very important in the past as it was used by both First Nations and settlers for building birch bark canoes. Presently, white birch wood is used extensively to make furniture as it can be stained to imitate more expensive wood. It is also used for flooring and interior trim. Locally, white birch only grows to the quality and size for use as firewood.

5 Gardiner (Mile 18.6)

To the east (right) of the train, you will observe what remains of a privately owned mill that was used to process locally harvested wood for the now defunct Quebec and Ontario Paper Company Ltd. The area is now used as a landing for present-day forestry operations. Trees were cut by local contractors, brought to the mill and bucked into 2.4 metre (8 feet) lengths, peeled (bark removed), then loaded onto specially designed pulpwood rail cars. Approximately 700 rail car loads per year were shipped to the company's pulp and paper mill on the Niagara Peninsula in Thorold, Ontario. The mill in Gardiner was built in 1979 and processed approximately 19,500 cords ($70,792m^3$) per year until it closed in the fall of 1987. Seven men were employed per shift, with two shifts per day. Over the nine year period during which the mill operated, approximately 176,000 cords ($637,128m^3$) of wood were obtained from the 9,106 hectares (22,500 acres) harvested. The area was regenerated by planting and aerially seeding black spruce and jack pine and some was left to regenerate naturally.

6 Poplar Stand (Mile 22)

Pure poplar stands line both sides of the tracks. Poplar reaches maturity between 60 and 80 years of age, attaining an average height of 25 to 30 metres (82 to 98 feet) and an average diameter of 30 to 40 centimetres (12 to 16 inches). Poplar requires full sunlight in order to regenerate and grow. The majority of poplar regeneration occurs from shoots which sprout from roots and stumps once the tree is cut or killed by fire, insects, or disease. Poplar is a favourite food of the beaver, which eat the bark and then use the small trees and branches to build lodges. Poplar buds are also a favourite food of the Ruffed Grouse.

7️⃣ Black Spruce Stands (Mile 26.1, 27.5, 29, 30.3)

As you continue to travel north, you will notice black spruce stands, some burned, on both sides of the train. These stands originated between 1900 and 1920. Black spruce is a coniferous tree that can be recognized by its tall spindly shape, a characteristic cluster of branches at the top, widely spaced branches down the remainder of the stem, and drooping branches that turn up at the ends. The cluster of branches at the top resembles a club from a distance. White spruce trees may be seen scattered throughout these stands. From a distance, white spruce has a pronounced cone shape and more branches. Traditionally, spruce roots were used by First Nations to sew the seams of birch bark canoes.

Spruce is the most common tree species in Ontario and is found across the province up to the limit of tree growth in the far north. Approximately half of the black spruce stands found in the boreal forest grow on wet, peatland, or swampy sites. On this type of site, black spruce is usually the only tree species present. The remaining black spruce stands grow on drier, upland sites, either by themselves, or mixed with other tree species. Both black and white spruce are able to regenerate and grow in the shade but best growth occurs in full sunlight. Large continuous stands of pure black spruce are very common in the boreal forest of northern Ontario. This is the result of forest fires which removed previous stands and allowed black spruce to become established.

In the Cochrane area, black spruce reaches maturity between 90 and 120 years of age. It achieves an average diameter of 20 to 30 centimetres (8 to 12 inches) and an average height of 9 to 15 metres (30 to 50 feet). On the tundra and bogs north of Moosonee, it is often dwarfed to a mere shrub. Black spruce grows well on moist cool soils. On sites covered with moss, it often regenerates by layering *(a lower branch becomes buried in the moss, grows new roots, and may develop into a new tree)*. Otherwise, new trees develop from seeds released from its cones.

White spruce, in the Cochrane area, mature between 90 and 120 years of age, attaining an average diameter of 45 centimetres (18 inches), and an average height of 20 to 24 metres (65 to 80 feet). It grows best on well drained soils. Spruce is economically important to both the lumber and the pulp and paper industry in Ontario. Spruce lumber is used for general construction, interior finishing, plywood, and crates. Spruce wood is almost tasteless and odourless and is the preferred material for food containers. Its natural light colour and desirable fibre characteristics (length and strength) make spruce the most valuable tree species in the world for paper production.

Mature spruce stands are a preferred winter habitat for moose, as the density of this forest type can reduce snow accumulation beneath the trees, making it easier for the moose to travel. The winter winds are also reduced which makes it warmer than other forest types. Spruce forests are also the preferred habitat of many species of birds such as the Boreal Chickadee, Spruce Grouse and Sharp-tailed Grouse. The Connecticut Warbler, which is much sought-after by bird watchers, flourishes in this forest type.

8 Tamarack (Mile 39.1 – 39.7)

On both sides of the train you will see coniferous trees with light green needles. These are tamarack, also known as larch, and are seen here at different ages mixed with spruce trees (dark green needles). The older tamarack were established around 1890 to 1900. Tamarack is the only coniferous tree in Ontario whose needles turn yellow and actually fall off each autumn. In the winter, the trees look dead, but they grow new soft needles every spring. Tamarack are found throughout Ontario accompanying the spruces to the limit of tree growth in the far north. They grow in wet cold soils, occasionally in stands by themselves, but usually mixed with black spruce. Tamarack require full sunlight to regenerate and grow.

This tree species reaches maturity between 90 and 120 years of age, attains an average diameter of 20 to 30 centimetres (8 to 12 inches), and an average height of 15 to 20 metres (50 to 65 feet).

[9] Island Falls (Mile 44.4)

You are crossing the Abitibi River for the second time during this trip. The Abitibi, as well as the Mattagami River, which is located several kilometres west of the rail line, are part of a massive system called the Moose River Drainage Basin. Collectively, these rivers drain an area of approximately 10,000 square kilometres (3,860 square miles) northward into James Bay. The basin extends from north of Sudbury right to James Bay, and from east of Lake Superior to the Quebec-Ontario border. Historically, this massive area has and continues to be very important to our First Nation people and their livelihood. Fifteen hydroelectric generating stations presently exist on the Abitibi and Mattagami Rivers, but only two, both located on the Abitibi River, can be seen from the train as we journey north. One of these is the Island Falls station which was built in 1925. It is located on the east side of the tracks. Watch for the impressive Otter Rapids station, built in 1958, as we cross the river again at mileage 93.5.

[10] Mileage Signs (Mile 45)

The mileage signs have now switched from the east (right) side of the train to the west (left) side of the train.

[11] [12] [13]   Forest Fires (Mile 49 – 67.1)

On both sides of the rail line for the next 18 miles, you will notice a mosaic of forest stands and vegetation patterns within a relatively young forest. A series of fires in the mid-1970's and 1980's was the cause of this patchwork of young regenerating forest permeated by small islands and pockets of older surviving trees. In 1976, a fire burned most of the area between mile 49 and mile 53.5. Firefighters, helicopters, and water bombers battled the blaze for six weeks until it was brought under control. The cost of fighting this fire, at the time, was $271,000!

Once again, the effects and influence of wildfire are evident on both sides of the train between mile 56.2 and mile 58.1. This fire occurred in 1986 consuming 915 hectares(2,260 acres) of timber.

Old burns like this remind us of the damage that forest fires can cause in terms of human values. Careless campers and improperly extinguished cigarettes are still a major cause of forest fires in Ontario. Lightening is also a common cause.

Please be careful while traveling or camping...

On both sides of the train between miles 60 and 67.1, you may notice the remnants of yet another old fire. In 1977, firefighters battled the blaze that occurred here for three weeks until it was finally extinguished after having consumed 1,821 hectares (4,500 acres) of forest land.

Wildfire is a common and natural occurrence in the boreal forest. Prior to the 1940's, extensive fires swept through this area every 100 to 150 years! The boreal forest depends upon fire to release nutrients into the soil and promote new growth, resulting in a vibrant healthy forest, and creating a mixture of essential wildlife habitats that are vital for maintaining biodiversity!

Fire in itself is really neither good nor bad but is deemed so depending on what human values are affected. Since the early 1940's, unwanted fires in the area have and continue to be controlled in order to protect human life, property, wildlife, and timber resources.

14 Harvested Areas (Mile 70.8)

The area to the east (right) side of the train was harvested during the summer and fall of 1990; five separate areas were harvested totalling 290 hectares (717 acres). The majority of trees harvested were black spruce. Subsequently, the area was aerial seeded in the spring of 1991 at a rate of 50,000 seeds per hectare in a regulated drop from an airplane. The regeneration has been highly successful!

The majority of stands in the boreal forest actually originate from fire! Historically, fire has regularly consumed thousands of hectares of continuous boreal area, and this has resulted in corresponding natural regeneration of large continuous stands containing one dominant tree species following these massive fires. Forest ecosystems thrive on large disturbances, such as fire, allowing natural regeneration and enhancing wildlife habitat. Harvesting operations, which remove most usable trees and leave some residual patches of trees, are an attempt to mimic natural conditions following a fire. Harvest areas are purposely configured to various shapes and sizes, with the most common form being an irregular pattern, often determined by terrain, and tree species and age. Forest regeneration often involves some form of site preparation (the disturbance of the forest floor and topsoil to create suitable conditions for regeneration) and tending (controlling competing vegetation) of the new forest crop. This perpetuates an even-aged forest such as those often found naturally in the boreal forest.

15 Black Spruce Monocultures (Mile 81)

The black spruce you see on both sides of the rail line were established between 1870 and 1890. Following a disturbance such as fire, black spruce regenerates naturally in large stands, mixed with very few other tree species, becoming a monoculture stand. These two stands originated from fire and are typical of the black spruce you see anywhere in the boreal forest. They are relatively small, totalling 150 hectares (370 acres), but they are adjacent to hundreds of hectares of other similar stands. Black spruce, as well as jack pine, poplar, and white birch will all naturally regenerate to produce large monoculture stands.

16 Jack Pine Regen - After and Before! (Mile 86, 90)

On both sides of the train, you will see standing dead trees among young jack pine, a species that is second only to spruce in terms of economic importance to Ontario's forest sector, approximately 50 per cent is harvested for lumber and the other 50 per cent is used in pulp and paper production. Jack pine grows across Ontario but reaches its northern limit at about this latitude. It is coniferous and grows best on relatively dry sandy soils.

Jack pine naturally regenerates in large stands containing trees all the same age. Its cones are serotinous which means that they require temperatures of 63 degrees Celsius (145 degrees Fahrenheit) to open; *temperatures which result from fire or on very hot sand in summer...* The fire that regenerated these young jack pine occurred in the mid-1990's. At about mile 90, you will begin to see the older unburned jack pine that previously occupied the entire area. Jack pine requires full sunlight to regenerate and grow. Again, we see how fire is actually a natural component of

boreal forest ecosystems. In the Cochrane area, jack pine reaches maturity between 60 and 80 years of age and occurs only in small quantities due to lack of suitable growing sites. It attains an average diameter of about 30 to 40 centimetres (12 to 16 inches), and an average height of 15 to 20 metres (50 to 66 feet).

17 Otter Rapids (Mile 93.5)

To the east (right) of the train you will see the impressive Otter Rapids hydroelectric generating power station located on the Abitibi River. (Refer back to # 9 - mile 44.4 for further discussion).

18 Original James Bay Beaches (Mile 94 – 96)

You are now traveling across what were once some of the original James Bay beaches. James Bay was much larger following the retreat of the last glacier approximately 10,000 years ago. These 'raised' or 'relict' beaches are located at the northern edge of the Precambrian Shield and on the southern edge of the James Bay Lowland, once covered by a continental ice sheet which reached depths of 1500 to 3000 metres (5000 to 9000 feet) thick. The weight of this ice was enough to actually compress the land. Following the final retreat of the glaciers, the ground began and continues to rise through a process known as *'isostatic rebound'*. The waters of James Bay once covered this entire area, but as the land has risen, the water retreated northward to its present location. The sand on the beach ridges create suitable sites for jack pine.

19 Eastern White Cedar (Mile 100)

On the east (right) side of the train, you will observe a few small patches of eastern white cedar trees. This medium-sized tree grows in both swamps and on some upland sites across Ontario, extending north to James Bay. It often regenerates in pure stands but is also found mixed with other tree species. Eastern white cedar will regenerate and grow in the shade. Locally, eastern white cedar reaches maturity between 80 and 120 years, attaining an average diameter of 20 to 30 centimetres (8 to 10 inches), and an average height of 15 to 20 metres (50 to 65 feet). Wood from the eastern white cedar is light, soft, and very durable. Because of its resistance to rot, it has always been a favourite for posts, poles, shingles, canoes, and railway ties. Locally, cedar is not harvested commercially but is used by individuals on a relatively small scale.

19 Growth Influence of Black Spruce by Drainage
20 (Mile 100 - 110) (Mile 128 – 130)

A stand of black spruce dominates the land on both sides of the rail line for many miles. These trees are relatively ancient and were established between 1850 to 1870. Some of these very old spruce are only two to three metres in height, their growth having been stunted in the poorly drained black spruce wetlands that are starting to occur more frequently as we continue to travel north.

You may also notice that the black spruce tend to be taller the further they grow from the rail line itself. These larger trees are actually established along the shores of the Abitibi River to the east and the Mattagami River to the west. The greater growth rate which is evident in the trees along the rivers is a direct result of improved drainage provided by the rivers and their tributaries, which ultimately allows more oxygen to be available in the soil for use by the root systems. These roots require an unencumbered supply of oxygen in order to function properly.

21 Tamarack Trees (Mile 139 – 141)

Small branches taken from the tamarack trees, seen with black spruce on both sides of the train, are used by First Nations artisans living in area communities. The fine branches are gathered during the fall, winter, and spring months when they have no needles and are then used to create various beautiful and much sought-after craft items such as tamarack geese. The crafts made out of these branches are pleasantly aromatic when wet. See # 8 for more about tamarack.

22 Moose River (Mile 142.5)

The small community of Moose River, presently consisting of a few houses, is located at the junction of the ONR rail line and the Moose River. This is all that remains of a once thriving village which came into existence during the 1930's, when railway construction reached Moose River and construction of the longest

bridge on the entire ONR rail line, the 1,800 foot long Moose River bridge, was undertaken. It took the entire winter from October 1930 to May 1931 to complete this magnificent bridge. A camp was set up to house the rail workers and a general store was also opened. Prior to the arrival of the railway, the area had been used as a campsite by First Nations people traveling to and from their hunting and trapping grounds.

Logging around Moose River began in early 1932, following the completion of the rail line to Moosonee. With southern Ontario growing rapidly, building materials were in high demand Moose River was an ideal location to build a sawmill as the railway was now available to ship wood south and a large workforce, now unemployed due to the completion of the rail line, were in need of employment. Logging took place in the winter months as the land was too wet to work on when it was not frozen. Men cut down trees of useable size with axes and saws, removed the branches, and cut the trees into logs (usually 8 to 12 foot lengths), then used

horses to move the logs to the frozen rivers. The logs were stored on the river during the winter, floated down the river after the ice melted, and collected in the bay. Finally, the logs were hauled up the river bank to the sawmill where they were cut into lumber. Both the Missinaibi and the Mattagami rivers empty into the Moose River, which enabled a large area to be accessed for harvesting. In the fall of 1932, over one hundred men and their families were living in the community of Moose River. By 1940, the population had grown to approximately 300 people. Local First Nation people were also working for the sawmill, leaving their traditional hunting and trapping for a new way of life. Over the years, the accessible wood was depleted, and by the fall of 1953, the mill was shut down and people began moving away to seek employment elsewhere. All trees of useable size that could be accessed by waterways connecting the Moose River were harvested over this 21-year period. The trees that you now see either remained un-harvested during these past logging operations or became established in the intervening years. As you look over the forest that now thrives following extensive past harvesting, it is difficult to tell that this area was ever even disturbed!

23 Moosonee Area Forestry (Mile 186)

Most of the immediate Moosonee area and areas to the north lie within a vast region of discontinuous permafrost where patches of soil are frozen year round mixed with sites that thaw only in the summer. Approximately ten percent of the total of these northern areas are located within the permafrost zone where the soil is always frozen. These wild and isolated boreal expanses contain a mix of large and continuous stands of black spruce and tamarack, with huge fen complexes, slow-draining wetlands with grasses, shrubs, dwarf birch and tamarack, as well as large bogs, a wetland that usually contains black spruce and mosses, and where drainage does not occur. Where better drainage exists, usually along the edges of stream and river banks, white and black spruce, balsam fir, trembling aspen, balsam poplar, and white birch stands often occur.

Forestry along the Polar Bear Express

The area immediately surrounding Moosonee and Moose Factory was cleared of timber in the early 1900s when trees of useable size were harvested and hauled using sleighs pulled by horses during the winter months. From this original harvest, the wood was used for building and walkway construction, railway ties, and firewood. As the two communities grew, all trees and shrubs were cleared for approximately one kilometre around the town to help reduce any wildfire hazard from the surrounding bush. The trees, you now see surrounding Moosonee and Moose Factory, have become established since the original harvest and settlement in the early part of the last century. Due to slow tree growth resulting from restricted drainage and a short growing season, timber harvest in the area is now very limited. The best tree growth occurs immediately along the river banks as a result of improved drainage. The little wood that is harvested is limited to supplying local demand for fuel-wood and in the production of a small amount of lumber for building and construction.

We are interested in hearing from you.
If you have comments about this
publication, please drop us a line.

Lake Abitibi Model Forest, Box 129
Cochrane, Ontario
P0L 1C0

Phone: (705) 272-7810
Email: office@lamf.net
Visit us at: www.lamf.net

LAKE
ABITIBI

MODEL FOREST
NETWORK

RÉSEAU DE
FORÊTS MODÈLES

Ontario

Natural Resources
Canada

Canadian Forest
Service

Ressources naturelles
Canada

Service canadien
des forêts

Canada

Route of the
Polar Bear Express

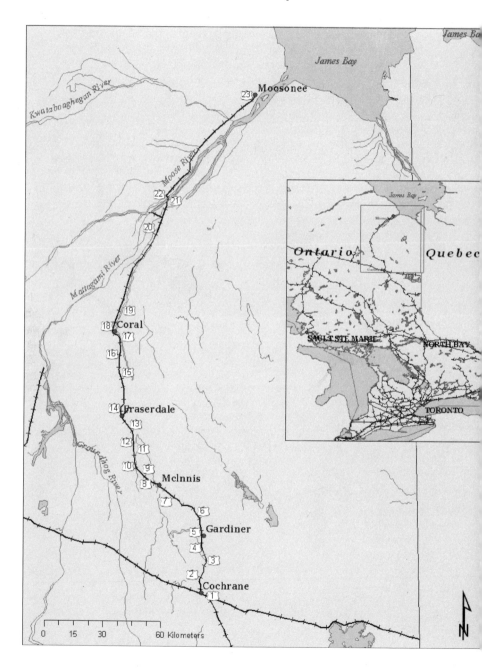

Ride the POLAR BEAR *Express*

CREDIT ONTARIO NORTHLAND

Pilot Ray Christman (left) and Cree pilot Terry McLeod sit at the controls of an Air Creebec deHaviland Dash-8 at Timmins awaiting air control instructions for a flight to James Bay.

MICHAEL BARNES

Visiting MOOSONEE and MOOSE FACTORY

Published by

GENERAL STORE
PUBLISHING HOUSE

499 O'Brien Rd., Box 415,
Renfrew, Ontario, Canada
K7V 4A6
Telephone (613) 432-7697 or 1-800-465-6072
www.gsph.com

ISBN 1-896182-48-8
Printed and bound in Canada

Cover re-design by Custom Printers of Renfrew Ltd.
Original layout and design by Derek McEwen

Canadian Cataloguing in Publication Data

Barnes, Michael, 1934 –
    Ride the Polar Bear Express : visiting Moosonee and Moose Factory

ISBN 1-896182-48-8

    1. Moose Factory (Ont.)–History. 2. Moosonee (Ont.)–History.
    3. Moose Factory (Ont.)–Description and travel.
    4. Moosonee (Ont.)–Description and travel. 5. Ontario
    Northland Railway–History. I. Title

FC3095.M687B37 1996   971.3'42   C96-900348-X
F1059.J3B37 1996

First Printing May 1996
Second Printing May 1998
Third Printing February 2001
Fourth Printing February 2005

This book is for

Bishop and Carol Hennessy

and

John and Wendy Kirk

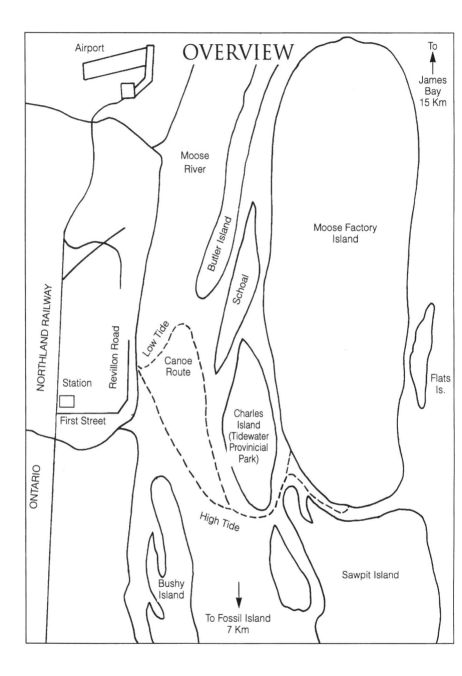

Contents

Michael Barnes.

Introduction

Northern Ontario is still very much the unknown land for most Canadians and certainly for visitors from other countries. The great wetlands of lower James Bay are even less known. Yet the area has an exciting past and an interesting present. Little more than three centuries ago the fur rich area around the great bays was the site of intense commercial rivalry and all-but war between the representatives of England and France. Hardly more than sixty years ago a railway link was forged with the rest of the province over some of the toughest ground in North America.

This book was suggested by the lack of more than pamphlet material on the two largest Cree settlements in Canada and certainly the largest places not hooked into the provincial highway system. The contents should be most helpful to tourists, business and government travellers and those who would like to fill in gaps in their knowledge of Canada. Those who intend to visit are advised to look over the section "Helpful Facts" first.

This book is more than a guide to the bottom of James Bay. It is a story of the Cree, the First Nation in this still-lonely land and the people who came after to make their home on the banks of the Moose River.

Sunset on the Moose River, 1936.

Smoked fish is still cured in a tipi in the old-time way.

1

The Early Land and its People

ONTARIO is the most populous, the richest and second-largest of the Canadian provinces. The name Ontario means beautiful lake or water. This Iroquois word is apt because more than one-sixth of its mass is rivers or lakes. The total area of Ontario is one million square kilometres and nine-tenths of that lies north of North Bay.

Northern Ontario is sparsely populated. There are only five cities and even the largest of these has not much more than 110,000 people. For the most part the towns in the north country have 10,000 or fewer residents.

The land mass of this huge, lonely land is close to one-tenth of Canada. It has two distinct regions. The greater is to the south and is made up of the Precambrian rocks of the Canadian Shield. This area is rich in minerals and forest land, but the Hudson Bay Lowlands that fringe Hudson and James Bays consist of bogs and shallow soils.

Cochrane, 423 kilometres north of Toronto, sits in the Great Clay Belt which cuts across northern Ontario and Quebec. Halfway between Cochrane and Moosonee is the southern limit of one of the greatest wetlands of the world. The Hudson Bay Lowlands are sometimes called the Great Swampy Muskeg. This is an area of poor drainage because the average land slope is only one metre in every kilometre. The cold weather which grips this area for more than half the year slows organic decay, and peat as much as two metres thick is formed. Fossils discovered in the area of Coral Rapids show that once this area was covered by a tropic sea. During the great ice age, millions of tons of glacial ice crushed the land. When the ice was gone, the land started to rise and it has been doing so ever since.

North of Cochrane on the Ontario Northland Railway line, the forest cover gives way to a land whose character is determined by water. Four-fifths of the Hudson Bay Lowlands consists of bogs, marshes, swamps and ponds. Long grasses alternate with stands of black spruce, lichens and tamarack. No wonder Canada geese, ducks, shore birds, mink and otter are plentiful in this remote region. Migratory birds favour the shallow mud flats of the great bays. Ringed, bearded and harbour seals, beluga whales and walrus are found along the shores.

Great rivers flow into the Arctic tidewater of James Bay. The Missinaibi, Mattagami and Abitibi rivers come together to form the Moose River. In total, the brown, mud-tinged waterway is about 563 kilometres long and as much as a kilometre wide in some places. The last thirty-five kilometres of this great river system are tidal. The twice-daily ebb and flow of the flood can make a difference of two metres. Travel and commerce are governed by the tide. Between Moosonee and Moose Factory, for example, low tide can add more than a kilometre to a freighter canoe trip between communities as boatmen detour to avoid low shoals and sandbars.

This great, lonely, largely-unknown country did not have its first human visitors until the last great glacial flows finally retreated eight to ten thousand years ago. The first people were nomads, ancestors of those we know today as the Swampy Cree. They came originally with others over the land bridge which once joined Alaska and Siberia. Even these hardy souls did not settle for several generations, but first made camps for summer use, for the area then was hardly suitable for permanent settlement. The muskeg made overland travel next to impossible for these early goose hunters, so those who eventually did stay year-round adapted by using canoes in the warm months and snowshoes and toboggans when the land was gripped by cold. Wildfowl and fish were the staple diet of these pioneer northerners.

The first people adapted to the land by banding together in social groups. The first chiefs were skilled hunters who took charge in the food-gathering times. A loose trade network among these early groups followed when they had grown accustomed to making shelter and finding food. The first Cree people later went further afield and bartered furs, meat and soapstone in exchange for tobacco and other items.

The Cree of the great muskeg believed that in the land they had the gifts of the Creator. The necessities of life could be found in the area so the waters and living things were held in trust for future generations. Only with the advent of a major imperial European trading organization did the Cree change their way of life. An existence which had depended solely on the provisions of nature encountered imported, manufactured goods. This began not much more than three hundred years ago.

Moose Fort, 1686.

D'Iberville storming Moose Fort .

Visitors to the Hudson Bay Company manager's house, 1890.

Moose Factory, 1854.

2

The Battle for James Bay

THREE CENTURIES ago the lonely waters of James and Hudson Bays and the rivers that run into them were the scene of a struggle for empire. Men did die by the cutlass, musket and cannon, but more often the harsh nature of the land took its toll. Tides, wind and weather have always been formidable opponents of those who move in to make the lowlands their home.

Early visitors came by sea and were not tourists. They were explorers seeking a passage to the east. All suffered in the attempt and only a few are remembered, mainly through their names on waters, straits or peninsulas. Henry Hudson died after being cast adrift by a mutinous crew. Captain Thomas James was probably the first European to reach the bottom of James Bay in 1631. He left his name there and also named the cape Henrietta Maria.

Renegade French explorers and fur traders Radisson and Groseilliers were advance men for a newly formed Company of Gentlemen Adventurers Trading into Hudson Bay. The Hudson Bay Company received its royal charter in 1671 and in January of the following year had men on the bays. Radisson went as far as "Moose Cebee... a broad river about eighteen leagues off the banks whereof are furnished with straight and tall trees of pine and spruce fit for masts..."

Trading with the Cree people began, but it was not until 1673

Hudson Bay docks, Moose Factory, 1900.

that the first governor, Charles Bayly, erected a small house upstream from the mouth of the Moose River. The ship *Wivenhoe* brought "some bricks and nayles to serve for erection of the forte..." By 1674 fur pelts were shipped from "Fort Mousipi... at the bottom of the Bay." Bayly stayed for six years. He was a man of culture and relieved "the cold days and long winter nights in a desolate part of the world... with a violl and shell and strings."

The Muskikegowuk or Swampy Cree who met the first European visitors were still nomads. They carried their few possessions to hunting and fishing grounds. They spent summers on the rivers and lakes, while in the snow season they moved inland to hunt and trap. The *meegwam*, a tent of skins, evolved as portable dwelling and snowshoes and toboggans were developed for winter travel. The Cree groups made community decisions by consensus. Decisions affecting the lives of all were subject to much discussion.

The Cree were shaped by their religious beliefs. Nature was respected and food sources were conserved as a result. Scapulimancy was used by shamen or spiritual leaders to guide hunters in their search for game. This was a form of divination, where the shoulder blade of a recently killed caribou was held over a fire and interpreted to locate good hunting areas.

The Hudson Bay Company soon came to realize that trade, not a passage to the east, would make profits for shareholders. No one knew that the charter given by Prince Rupert turned four-tenths of Canada over to a commercial group. Twenty years after its founding, the Honourable Company tripled its capital and continued for close to three hundred years to give handsome returns on investment. But from 1686 there was a period of trade uncertainty. This was due to an attack on the English monopoly from an unexpected quarter.

The bottom of the bay was the target of one of the most successful commando-type raids ever undertaken on the continent. While the English came by sea, the French made their incursions from their colonies along the St. Lawrence River. Colonial leaders first heard reports of English ships on James Bay from Father Albanel in 1672, and in 1679 Louis Joliet confirmed much activity there. While the English built forts and waited for trappers to come to them, the French sent canoemen, *coureurs de bois*, hard-living, energetic "runners of the woods," to trade directly with their customers.

The Hudson Bay Company was a private enterprise, but in

Moose Factory, circa 1870.

effect the French fur trade operation was an extension of government. The colonial administration financed operations by taxes on the fur trade. The English brought goods in volume on ocean-going ships while the French took light loads by canoe containing only the most popular consumer items. In this way they could respond to changing needs, although staple trade goods remained muskets, powder and ball, kettles, knives, tobacco and brandy.

Radisson and Groseilleurs were not popular with their countrymen because they had changed allegiance in the fur trade to

After the sleigh run, Hudson Bay Company compound, 1905.

Trading Post Manager Dick Ward and Capt. Joe Neilson.

OA 16289-22

Tipis set up for the annual Treaty Day celebrations, 1920s.

OA 11509

Sunday finery for the annual Treaty Day. The Hudson Bay staff house, background, and the guns remain today.

the English masters who paid a higher living. When in 1684 Radisson captured Fort Charles and it became Rupert's House in the English service, the governor of New France, Jacques de Brisay, found an excuse to wipe out the English presence on the bays.

In 1686 he sent 107 men north. There were six officers, a chaplain, thirty colonial soldiers and seventy canoemen, who were similar to a militia unit today. Leader Pierre de Troyes was said to have "wit, wisdom, prudence and savoire faire." De Troyes was a good improviser and planner and said of his ragtag gang of canoemen that *les Canadiens* had a character which hardly accorded with submission. Two of his officers were the Le Moyne brothers. One, Pierre, Sieur d'Iberville, became a popular soldier of fortune later.

Hudson Bay Company schooner Otter, circa 1920.

The daring party travelled at a tough time of year, and it was ten weeks before they were in a position to attack the English traders. They set out March 30, 1686, and went up the Ottawa and Mattawa Rivers to Lake Timiskaming, then along the White River to the Abitibi River and Lake Abitibi. The party of ten canoes had many natural obstacles to overcome en route. It was break-up time in several areas so they had to detour around ice, navigate lengthy portages and rapids, continually repair canoes, and even avoid a forest fire at one point. The close of their epic journey was plagued by black flies, but by June 15th the party was close by Moose Fort.

D'Iberville reconnoitered the area. He noted the fur fort was on a large island in the Moose River. The forty-metres-square palisade was built of five-metre-high logs and there were small three-cannon bastions at each corner. The three-level building or redoubt in the centre was defended by four cannon. The only entrances were a large door at the front and a small sally port at the rear. De Troyes planned to attack with rough ladders and dispersed his men carefully. Some stayed near the gate with a home-made battering ram, others made ready their ladders near the walls, while reserves stayed back to cover their comrades.

D'Iberville was first man into the fort after the ram splintered the door. Faced with the early-morning swarm of men over the walls and through the door, the English settlers did not put up an effective resistance. The attack was over in half an hour, prisoners secured on an old ship moored in the river, and the party was off to the next targets.

Today a flight over the almost-contourless veined mass of islands, sandbars and streams reveals how well the De Troyes party did despite their lack of knowledge of the area. The southern adventurers captured Rupert's House after a fierce struggle and took cannon on a ship seized there. By July 26th the hard-driving leader had successfully carried out his mission by capturing Fort Albany after a short battle. The party returned to a rousing welcome in Montreal seven months after setting out, having overcome bad weather, rough terrain and little food, and having lost only three men.

De Troyes never repeated his success on James Bay. In 1687 he was placed in charge of Fort Niagara but lost ninety percent of his complement in a harsh winter due to scurvy. The innovative adventurer perished because he did not seek assistance from the

OA 16259-13

Semi-annual mail packet about to leave Moose Factory on ten-day trip to Cochrane, 1923.

OA 14150-11

A pensive employee of the James Bay Fur Company, 1925.

OA 16723

Horses protected from flies by muslin covers, Moose Factory, 1929.

OA 16723

The doctor's ship leaving Moosonee, 1925.

PA 99582

The Hudson Bay Company manager's house and waterfront at Moose Factory, 1926.

native people or use common sense. But his accomplishment was recognized by his superiors. He had shown that the best way to come to the bays was by sea, since the overland route was not suitable for large-scale movement of goods.

The Hudson Bay Company profit-taking was actually slowed for about twenty-seven years. The posts on the bay see-sawed back and forth between the English and French during that period. At one point the complex on the Moose River became Fort Ste. Anne, was retaken by its former owners and then recaptured by d'Iberville. Nasty rumour has it that the soldier of fortune was glad to be fighting in the north country because he had a paternity suit hanging over his head back home. The alarms on James Bay ended in 1713 at the Treaty of Utrecht, when the English recovered their fur trade forts.

The Hudson Bay Company was a great firm for paper and from its voluminous records we have a clear picture of life at Moose Fort from that time forward. The company had strict regulations and factors or managers had guidelines for most occasions. Apart from a splurge of food and drink at Christmas time, with local provisions and rations sent from England, life was hard throughout the year. In

PA 62884

Airplanes first arrived on James Bay in 1921. Famous visitor Charles Lindburgh with his wife on their honeymoon Orient flight at Moose Factory, 1931.

PA 6220668

Fokker Super Universal Fairchild at Moose Factory, late thirties.

In 1935 the attic of the Hudson Bay Store held a wealth of treasures.

1731 a cook left a grease pot on the stove and the post burned down. Tough factor James Duffield, sent out in 1741, strengthened discipline by lashing offenders to the stove so that they would be the first to perish if carelessness caused fire.

The big event each year for fur trade posts was the annual visit of the supply ship. The goods in the ship's hold gave the Cree a chance for a better life. Ice chisels, axes, copper pans, fish hooks, guns, powder and shot, knives, files and cloth were welcome trade items. The ships also brought tough islanders, Orkneymen from the north of Scotland, who would work as company servants in the trade. As many as twenty-five served at Moose Fort for many years. They came and learned from the Cree. The use of canoes, toboggans and snowshoes was invaluable and they used practical moccasins and made pemmican for occasional trips outside the area.

Moose Factory was the hub for the direction and supply of southern posts. Under the factor were the officers, termed commissioned gentlemen and addressed as Mister. When such men arrived or departed from any post, they were entitled to a cannon shot in salute. But behind the pomp was a lonely life for these men so far from home, and many turned to rum for solace during long winter nights.

The Cree trappers provided the most sought-after furs: the thick, lustrous beaver pelts. This fur was eagerly sought in Europe where it could be easily shaped, sometimes for coats, but generally for hats for men. The popular furs were referred to as "made beaver" or MB in fur trade shorthand. The pelts even became the accepted currency in the north. One MB could purchase two metres of cloth, five kilograms of shot, four litres of brandy or almost a kilogram of nails. A pistol changed hands at four made beaver while a musket traded for three times that amount.

After 1803 the North West Company set up business on Hayes Island just across from Moose Factory, but within three years the Honourable Company had undersold the traders it called "peddlers" and they were gone. All information was considered secret by the masters of the fur trade. They would not give out details of tide fluctuations and even adopted a company calendar. Each year was numbered as an investment since the virtual monopoly was started. The year 1996, for example, would be "outfit 326" in company records.

For most of the nineteenth century Hudson Bay Company operations sliced up Canada into four sections for administration. Moose Factory was the base of the southern portion and for a while one of the most powerful men in the country lived there. Sir George Simpson ruled the trading empire in Canada. Called "the Little Emperor" in an allusion to Napoleon and his stature, Simpson wielded tremendous power.

The Hudson Bay Company dominated the Moose Factory scene in 1935.

The earliest ship to arrive at Moose Fort between 1751 and 1880 arrived in 1834 on July 25th. The vessel must have closely skirted the retreating ice. Normally the supply vessels arrived in August, and after a week to unload goods and pick up the fur pelt harvest, upped anchor and were gone for another twelve months. Their masters did not want to be caught in the bays and face the vagaries of fall weather.

One of the many famous men who spent time at the bottom of the bay was Doctor John Rae, later to be a great Arctic explorer. For ten years he received 100 pounds per annum to minister to the sick. He also conducted scientific expeditions and travelled through the bush with the Cree. His employer even used him for Arctic explorations and he branched out on a search for evidence of the ill-fated Franklin expedition. He spent six years at it and a grateful British government rewarded him with ten thousand pounds, far more than he ever received from the Honourable Company.

Gradually the Cree people changed their way of life and moved to settle around the company trading posts. Some company servants intermarried with First Nations people and a Métis, or people of mixed blood, was established. The notion of defence for the posts was abandoned and company servants often lived outside the posts in their own log houses, without title to the land.

The Wesleyans were the first missionaries to preach in the area, arriving in 1840, but in 1850 John Horden led the vanguard of the Church of England, now the Anglican Church of Canada. He spent his life there, became first Bishop of Moosonee in 1872, and even adapted James Evans' system of syllabic symbols to the Cree language. Now the people could read and write in their own tongue. Horden's original church, St. Thomas, still stands at Moose Factory. The residential school the hard working bishop successfully lobbied governments to build served its purpose and is long gone but the present hospital and school simply follow from earlier church efforts to establish these facilities.

Trade was still strong on the bay and in 1884 $100,000 was collected on Moose Factory Island in customs duties alone. In that year a government official sent north on a fact-finding mission suggested the appointment of a constable, the negotiation of a treaty with the Cree and even more power for the Hudson Bay Company. Two years later the whole island was ceded to the fur trade monopoly without consultation with the Cree people, who

For many years children came by boat from coastal communities to go to school at Moose Factory. Below decks on the RC Mission ship Nouveau Quebec.

did not get the treaty they sought until another twenty years had passed.

At the turn of the century there were 571 persons on Moose Factory Island, of whom 193 were company employees or dependents. The rival fur company, Revillon Frères, set up shop on the mainland in 1903. This may be seen as the founding of Moosonee. The newcomers were welcomed by the Cree for they provided an element of competition, but within thirty years the well-entrenched Hudson Bay Company had won the local trade battle. But one tradition ended: ocean-going ships ceased to come to the mouth of the Moose River. Instead, they dropped anchor at Charlton Island and smaller vessels ferried goods up the river.

Poet and civil servant Duncan Campbell Scott brought a federal treaty party to the bay in 1905. There was great ceremony and feasting but all the group did was listen to their hosts and then dictate the terms of the treaty. The Cree gave up their lands— roughly 233,100 square kilometres—in return for the promise of schools and medical services. Traditional hunting rights were retained, reserve lands were assigned, and each band member was to receive four dollars annually. It was a deal which native leadership bitterly regretted later.

The settlement at the bottom of the bay was still isolated in the early twentieth century. The nearest town of Cochrane was a journey of eight to ten days south. The area still depended on supply ships from the old country, but did have the benefit of one carefully-husbanded resource which is not so apparent today. The rich alluvial delta soil encouraged farming for it produced good crops of hay, grain, potatoes and other vegetables to complement the harvest of the seasonal goose hunt.

Aircraft ended the isolation on the Moose River. The first plane arrived in 1920 and on August 1, 1931, Charles Lindburgh and his bride stopped over on their way to the Orient. The famous flyer was a great hit in the area and to the present day the name Lindy is a popular choice for a new baby.

The years of isolation were effectively over when the Temiskaming and Northern Ontario Railway, now the Ontario Northland, arrived at the new townsite of Moosonee. Lots were expensive, running to $25 for residences and up to $750 for a business location. The railway had been sought as a social necessity but its construction and operation was to vex governments for years to come. There were few natural resources north of the divisional point of Cochrane to pay its way, and it was generally subsidized by revenues from more profitable sections of the line. The arrival of rail meant that supply ships for the fur trade were no longer needed. Soon the Hudson Bay Company district office moved to Winnipeg and its operations in the two communities were reduced to those of the trading posts.

The Cree served Canada with distinction in two World Wars and Korea. The institution of the Polar Bear Express train brought more visitors after World War II and tourism became an employment alternative to trapping and service jobs. In 1949 the fine Moose Factory General Hospital was opened. The Cross of Lorraine shape recalls the fight against tuberculosis, especially among northern natives. The disease is largely eradicated now, but the hospital, now known as Weeneebayko, remains busy and benefits from Queen's University medical staff who serve there on a rotating basis.

From the mid-sixties there was much activity at Moosonee due to the operation of the Mid-Canada Pinetree radar base. In the period of the Cold War, when it was in operation, the facility brought further jobs and prosperity to the head of steel. After the servicemen who served under the white radar domes were gone, much of the infrastructure remained.

From the sixties, Moose Factory was the more populous of the two communities. An expensive coal-fired heating plant served the island hospital. Coal came up by rail and was trucked over on winter ice roads. Newcomers could be forgiven for thinking the track of coal dust across the frozen river was paved blacktop.

The railway promoted Moosonee as an ocean port, pointing to area deposits of northern gypsum, limestone, lignite, china and fire clay, silica and the iron of the Belcher Islands to the north. But extensive silting of the river, due in part to the damming of the waterway upstream, plus the short shipping season on the bays, have prevented the idea of a port from becoming a reality.

Improvements for the aboriginal people over the past few years have included upgraded roads, water supply and sanitary services. The James Bay Education Centre was taken over by the Northern College of Applied Arts and Technology giving residents access to post-secondary education. The development of a secondary school at Moosonee meant that young people did not have to leave the support of family and friends and travel south in order to achieve their goals.

As for the venerable Hudson Bay Company, in a surprising move it quit the fur trade business altogether in the eighties. One result was a delicious piece of historical irony. A group of former managers bought out the northern stores and took for the new firm's name that of the original trade rival the Hudson Bay Company had put out of business in 1821. Now the operation is represented in both communities by the North West Company Northern Stores.

Historic Hudson Bay Company staff house at Moose Factory today.

3

The Railway Link with a Lonely Land

THE transcontinental Canadian Pacific Railway reached North Bay in 1882. It would be another twenty years before railway building headed north. During that time tourist promoters for the Temagami area and residents of New Liskeard and Haileybury pushed hard for a railway as there was no highway connection north. The clay belt lands 150 kilometres north of Lake Nipissing offered promise of rich farm land and settlement opportunities.

In 1900 the province sent ten survey teams north to map what was then known as New Ontario, mainly white areas on the map, as yet uncharted wilderness. The surveyors brought back accounts of huge timber stands, mineral deposits and countless lakes and rivers. When it was noted that a northbound rail system could connect with the National Transcontinental Railway—later the Canadian National—then being built, a decision was made to commence work on the Temiskaming and Northern Ontario Railway in 1902.

In its first six years the government railway pushed through some of the toughest terrain in the country to arrive at the probable connection point with the Transcontinental Railway in 1908. The town of Cochrane grew at this junction point, but by that time the railway, which billed itself as Ontario's development road, was paying its bills. A huge silver strike at Cobalt brought tremendous revenue to the T&NO Railway and with the addition of branch lines and huge gold strikes in the Porcupine (now Timmins) in 1909 and Kirkland Lake in 1912, government leaders could see they had made a wise investment in a railway that private enterprise could not be persuaded to build.

The head of steel remained at Cochrane until 1923 when prospects of resource development

George Lee, railway general manager (left), Ontario Premier G.Howard Ferguson (third from left), camping on the way to Moosonee, 1923.

and opening a port at Moosonee, plus the opportunities of hydroelectric power generation, finally prodded the province to move north to the Arctic tidewater. The first construction contract was let as far as the Abitibi River and a new method of surveying was of great help. A plane based at Cochrane flew ahead of the ground-based engineers charting the easiest path for the tracks.

The Premier's party en route to James Bay, 1923.

The official seal of approval was fixed on the project when Ontario Premier G. Howard Ferguson made an unprecedented trip to Moosonee with a small party of advisors including the Lieutenant Governor. By rail, canoe and sail boat the party went on past the Moose Rapids and arrived at Moose Factory. The Cree celebrated the arrival by making the adventuresome premier an honorary chief, designating him "one whom the people honour." He reciprocated this gesture by supporting the northern railway extension venture all the way.

Trestle at Island Falls, mile 73, 1927.

For some time the extension stopped, first at Island Falls and later at Moose River Crossing, due to financial and political problems faced by the province. Even when the line was not building, a mixed freight train operated to the head of steel and it became known (as a joke, because the train was quite slow and there

Trestle at Island Falls being filled with ballast, 1927.

were no big white bears) as the Polar Bear Express.

The difficulties running rails to Moosonee were many, and tested the government's determination. Building the T&NO Railway over clay and then muskeg was a continual round of clay cuts and muskeg fill. The soggy muskeg of the great northern swamps seemed bottomless. Some sections

Railway builder Harry McLean's rail car, Island Falls, 1930.

ANDERSON

needed several trainloads of long-hauled ballast. Rock fill disappeared beneath the surface in short order. Travellers today see the straight tracks north of Cochrane and do not realize how long it took to bridge the swamps.

As the rails moved north the province explored for natural resources. Drill holes were put down at Onakawana where lignite deposits had been known for half a century. Strip mining was considered for this plentiful deposit of wet coal. The problem in its recovery was that lignite is not far removed from peat and half of its consistency is water. There was a plan to make briquettes with the stuff but nothing came of it and the deposit still lies undeveloped in the lowlands, along with a huge deposit of gypsum near the Moose River.

Railway construction halted

ENGLEHART AND AREA MUSEUM

Above: The railway under construction at Coral Rapids, 1930.

Right: Laying tracks north of Coral Rapids, 1930.

ENGLEHART AND AREA MUSEUM

at Fraserdale for a long time and when it finally resumed, Harry Falconer McLean was the contractor for the last leg of the line. McLean was a master builder and was responsible for huge projects across Canada. He was justly considered eccentric: even his idea of a good time was to throw large sums of money out of hotel windows in small bills "to make people happy." Later he came back and built the huge Abitibi hydro electric project. He saluted his workers on the completion of all jobs by erecting a cairn depicting Rudyard Kipling's poem, the Sons of Martha. This was for those workers whose toil and sweat, and sometimes lives, went to create great enterprises.

The railway head of steel reached Coral Rapids in 1930. Although the area was covered with up to two metres of muskeg, geologists found deep deposits of coral, and embedded in the formation were fossilized shark's teeth. This proved to the geologists' satisfaction that the area was once covered by a tropical sea.

ENGLEHART AND AREA MUSEUM

Men working ahead of the track-layer close to the Moose River.

BILL CHURCH

Once the supports were built, steel crossed the Moose River rapidly.

The CBC broadcast the opening of the line to Moosonee. Seen left of the microphone is railway General Manager George Lee.

The Great Depression ravaged the continent as the railway moved forward in 1930. Yet there was humour even in those hard times. The job seekers had special names for three northern trains. There was the Whisky Express from Quebec, so called because it brought gallons of bootleg liquor; the Doodlebug out of Kapuskasing; and south of Cochrane, the Galloping Goose. After World War II the Moosonee-bound trains became known as Polar Bear for the tourist train and Little Bear for the year-round mixed train.

Imagine you were with the party of visiting clergymen who were given a trip to the head of steel at Moose River Crossing in 1931. During the exciting trip by sedan fitted to travel the rails, the highlight was an overview of the construction at Abitibi Canyon. Here Harry McLean was building one of the great engineering projects in Canada. The clergy viewed the eleven-kilometre long canyon's 100-metre-high cliffs and huge horseshoe-shaped dam complex which would provide more than a quarter million electric horsepower. When the dam was complete, the United Church ministers were told, the river would be backed up for fifty-one kilometres.

One of the most impressive sights on the railway is the more-than-one-kilometre-long bridge across the Moose River. The crossing was effected at a cost of one million dollars in Depression-era money. Construction wizard Harry McLean planned the job very carefully. At this point the waters of the Missinaibi and Mattagami Rivers combine and circle an island. One channel had to be filled to provide a foundation and combat the power of the ice in spring break-up when its grinding abrasive power was enormous.

An embankment 630 metres long and twenty metres high had to be reinforced with earth from far south down the line, taking eight trainloads of sand and ballast. Two hundred men worked through the night by the light of flares when the attempt was made. The combination of ballast and 5,000 sand bags slowed the east channel to a trickle and finally stopped it.

Rails were laid and work started on the actual bridge. Everything had to be complete before the ice came churning down the river on its annual spring rampage. Concrete for fifteen piers and abutments were poured at extremely low temperatures. The separation of ingredients was prevented by a newly-developed method of pouring the mix through a horizontal canvas bag. There were seventeen spans; three spanned up to thirty-five metres. The Hamilton Bridge Company took only a month to erect the bridge steel and the rails soon followed.

The last seventy-four kilometres of line to Moosonee was completed quickly. The 125 invited guests to the last-spike ceremony at 10:30 a.m. on July 15, 1932, remarked on the great achievement of the railway when everywhere else progress had just about ground to a halt. Locals marvelled at the first car which came

ENGLEHART AND AREA MUSEUM

After 1932 the railway operated canoes between the mainland and Moose Factory.

to the tidewater equipped with skis at the front and tractor wheels at the rear.

A CBC radio microphone was set up in the middle of the tracks and Ontario Judge Frank Latchford, who had pounded the first spike in North Bay thirty years before, reprised his role and declared the line open to the public. Perhaps few at the ceremony realized that it was 300 years to the day since Captain James had sailed his tiny ship to the great bays seeking a new world.

The return fare to Cochrane on the new service was $6.45, but in those tough times few but business travelers could afford to make the trip. The power sites on the rivers had been developed but no one remarked that while railway expenditures were up almost fourteen percent, revenues in those lost years had decreased almost twenty-one percent.

Harry McLean built another of his cairns to the Sons of Martha at the entrance to Moosonee and a tourist lodge opened. Ontario now had a railway which made connections from Lake Ontario to the sub-Arctic. The long period of isolation for the settlements at the bottom of James Bay was over. Railway engineers were caught up in the excitement of the moment but acted prudently to protect the Moose River bridge. For many years they stationed a watchman there in the spring to observe any evidence of damage caused by the forces of ice and water.

The Big Bear, without its famous Polar Bear insignia, at Moosonee, 1979.

4

Down North on the Polar Bear Express

FOR just over ten weeks each summer from late June to the Labour Day weekend, the small northern Ontario town of Cochrane is swelled by an influx of visitors who arrive to take one of the last great romantic train rides left in North America. Cochrane is on Highway 11, one of the two trans-Canada road routes. Up to 600 people a day, six days a week, from Tuesday to Sunday, arrive at this small town to take the 186-mile trip to Moosonee on the sub-Arctic tidewater. A word about distance. While this book uses metric measure, the portion relating to the railway works with miles, for train travel is one of the last hold-outs of imperial measure.

The passengers carried by the provincial railway, the Ontario Northland, choose this excursion because their destination is not accessible by road. The four hour and twenty minute trip runs through a sparsely populated country of forests, lakes, rivers and just plain scrub bush and muskeg. The destination is worth the effort to make the trip. At the end of the line are the two largest isolated settlements in Ontario, the gateway to James and Hudson Bays and the oldest permanent English-speaking settlements in the province.

Some visitors are mislead by the train's name. The popular title dates from Depression-era times when the inference was that all travellers would see was the big white bears. Yet the nearest of these noble beasts are found at Cape Henrietta Maria in Polar Bear Provincial Park, far north of Moosonee. Nonetheless Cochrane has adopted the great white bear as an unofficial emblem. Including the big statue at the entrance to town, children could have fun counting how many times they see the bear symbol on their trip.

Visitors park their cars across from the historic Cochrane Union Station. It was built in 1908 after the Temiskaming and Northern Ontario Railway, predecessor of the present line, finished

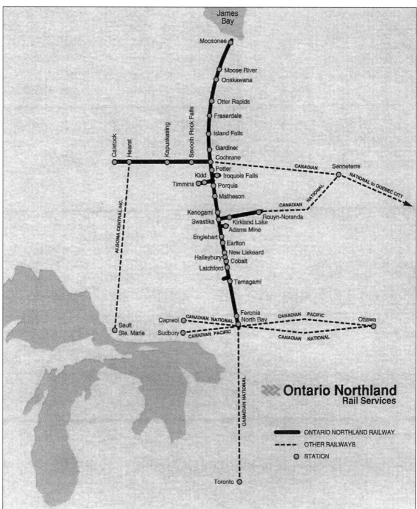

Making rail connections with the Ontario Northland.

its six-year track laying push from North Bay. The facade is much the same as it was when it sheltered people during the disastrous killer fires of 1911 and 1916 which swept northeastern Ontario. It is called Union Station because the National Transcontinental Railway, later Canadian National, crossed the tracks nearby and both lines used the same facility.

The station interior has been extensively modernized. In an innovative move in 1990, the railway raised the roof of the historic building and incorporated a hotel into the structure. Visitors who stay there will no longer hear the clang of the railway telegraph but will find all amenities, including a restaurant, plus a central location for exploring Cochrane.

Passengers congregate half an hour before train time behind a yellow line painted on the platform. The crowd is often big and this line keeps the throng back from the edge of the low platform. A wide variety of accents graces the gathering group. Cars and trailers in the parking lot represent a broad swath of Canadian provinces and American states and there will also be overseas travellers. Most are dressed sensibly in outdoor clothing and sturdy shoes, for their destination leads to some productive walking. Some wander into the souvenir shop housed in the former freight shed at the north end of the station.

The platform lacks the solemn atmosphere usually found in railway stations. There is an almost carnival air as railway personnel double as cartoon characters and entertain the crowd. These people change roles when the train moves north; they work on the trip as tour guides. The Polar Bear car make-up varies, but a typical run might have as many as sixteen units, including two dining cars—one 'take out' for snacks, which later doubles as a bar, and an entertainment car which at different times will serve both children and adults. The passenger cars are clean and comfortable and all riders are guaranteed a seat.

Up front in the engine cab the engineer mutters a terse "Head rolling," into his radio and gives two blasts on the air horn. The train gives an exploratory lurch and then gently eases out of the station. Most of the engines used on the excursion train have more than a million miles on the clock and some twice that number. But they have all safety features including the famous Dead Man's pedal. The driver keeps his foot on the pedal at all times. He can take off the pressure for up to six seconds, then a warning whistle

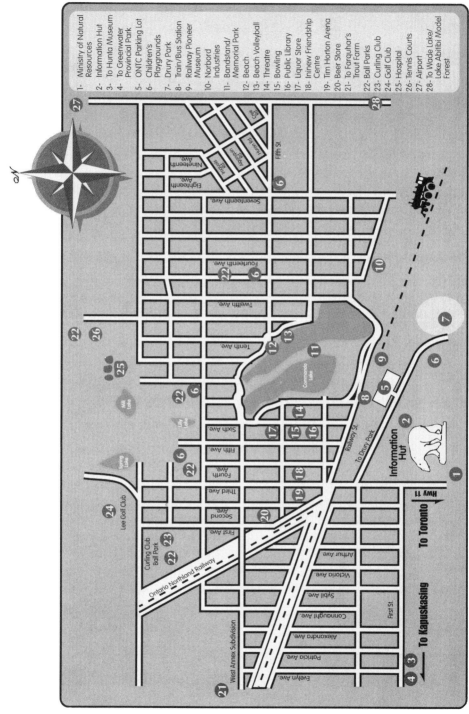

1- Ministry of Natural Resources
2- Information Hut
3- To Hunta Museum
4- To Greenwater Provincial Park
5- ONTC Parking Lot
6- Children's Playgrounds
7- Drury Park
8- Train/Bus Station
9- Railway Pioneer Museum
10- Norbord Industries
11- Bandstand/ Memorial Park
12- Beach
13- Beach Volleyball
14- Threatre
15- Bowling
16- Public Library
17- Liquor Store
18- Ininew Friendship Centre
19- Tim Horton Arena
20- Beer Store
21- To Farquhar's Trout Farm
22- Ball Parks
23- Curling Club
24- Golf Club
25- Hospital
26- Tennis Courts
27- Airport
28- To Wade Lake/ Lake Abitibi Model Forest

CREDIT: COCHRANE & AREA COMMUNITY DEVELOPMENT CORPN.

Cochrane today.

Sometimes the train engineer has a helper.

sounds. The big train will come to a stop unless pressure is exerted once more.

In railway terms – the expression railroad is more properly an American term – the territory covered to Moosonee is "black." This means that there are no block signals on this stretch. Engineers are always quick to quip that despite this lack, they know exactly where they are. The engineers have the best view on the train, but all travellers have an opportunity to see marsh hawks, red-tailed and rough-legged hawks, and ducks, including blacks, goldeneyes, canvasbacks and scaups (pronounced *skops*) or

Head end ready to roll.

bluebills. Bear, moose, beaver and even wood caribou appear by the tracks on occasion.

As the train picks up speed, alert window gazers will note the white mileage boards and indications of elevation. The height above sea level drops all the way down north; at Cochrane it is 261 metres while at the end of the line the figure stands at a mere 5.5 metres, hence the term "down north" rather than "up." Vegetation also changes en route. Spruce and poplar are the most common trees, along with the deciduous birch and tamarack. Known variously as the American larch, or *Hackamatack* in the Algonquin language, the tamarack has light feathery-green needles which turn yellow in the fall and then drop off. The bush abounds with wild orchids and tiger lilies and Labrador tea covers the swampy land.

The train takes on a rolling motion, reaching its average speed of forty-eight miles per hour as it covers the thirty-mile northern fringe of the great clay belt. This fertile farm land offers the last signs of commercial agriculture on the trip.

There will be some freight on the excursion train but the majority goes north on the

LORNE FLEECE

The rare curves on the Moosonee run mirror the train.

PAUL McLEOD

The Moosonee water tower with its distinctive Cree syllabics is one of the first – and last – glimpses train-bound visitors have of the end of steel.

ONTARIO NORTHLAND

Gliding into Moosonee.

year-round freight train. Goods marshalled in the Cochrane train yards can run the gamut from groceries, vehicles, fuel, spare parts for machinery, construction materials and even whole buildings. Not only Moose Factory and Moosonee benefit from the railway transport. Much of the freight is transshipped to communities further up the coast. Barges do the job in ice-free months and in winter tractor trains haul north over the frozen muskeg.

Mileage board 4.5 offers a glimpse of Lillabelle Lake, Cochrane's airport for bush float planes. Then at **mileage 11.4** riders have their first glimpse of the mighty Abitibi River. The muddy waters are quiet now, but this was one of the major fur trade routes of Canada and many famous Canadian fur traders and explorers dipped their paddles in its waters.

Just a little further on at **mileage 18.6**, Gardiner is indicated as the former site of a large logging operation. As many as 35,000 cords of black spruce were shipped annually from this point for southern newsprint plants. This wood is also used in the manufacture of ethyl alcohol and vanillin for flavours and also as an element of the pollution control system in paper mills. There will still be pulp cars to see at this location. Not far from this spot is Red Sucker River, a good fishing prospect.

The big train makes its way over the Little and Big Jawbone Rivers, which are named not for good conversation but for moose. Occasionally the engineer salutes a track-side hunt camp with an air horn blast. Gangs of yellow-hard-hatted section men work on the road bed. Those little blue sheds dotted at intervals along the right-of-way contain small wood shims to bring the rails level. Maybe one of the residents at Wurtelle will wave, but further on at Maher, there is nothing; it is just a name on the map now. Over Trapper's Creek, the train eases into Island Falls at **mileage 43**. The engineers up front like mileage boards because they are paid by distance worked.

The grade into Island Falls is steep. This used to be a concern in the days of steam as boiler water would rush to the front, leaving the back end dry. Now the diesels plug along despite fluctuations in the grade. The line reached this place in 1924. Just east of here is a 48,000 B.H.P. power station, the Abitibi River plant, which supplies power to the paper mill at Iroquois Falls, south of Cochrane. At **mileages 43, 93, 125 and 156** microwave towers are the only tall structures in the area. The provincial railway, not the familiar Bell Telephone, operates all telecommunications in this empty land. These 52-to-117-metres-high steel towers bring welcome radio and television for the area between Cochrane and Attawapiskat.

Once more the train crosses the Abitibi River and from **mileage 49.3 to 52** there are dead trees as far as the eye can see. This desolation is the legacy of a giant forest fire which destroyed 30,000 acres of timber in 1976. Water bombers and fire crews from across Canada and the United States took two weeks to bring the big burn under control. This was a fast-spreading tree-top or crown fire, one of the most difficult to bring under control. During the fire the mixed freight, the Little Bear, kept running, but each trip was hot and smoky for the crew.

Within another ten minutes the train reaches Fraserdale at **mileage 69.2**, the end of the road link with the south. The awesome size of the Abitibi Canyon, just 2.4 kilometres to the east, is best seen from the air. Each year it attracts tourists who take the road link from Highway 11 to view the huge power dam complex. The generators commenced working in 1933 and a quarter century later Ontario Hydro added four more stations on the Moose River system. Otter Rapids, Harmon and Kipling all send much-needed electricity south through the Pinard Transformer Station. The combined output of 761,100 kilowatts can power an industrial city the size of Hamilton. Once there was a model community of 350 people here, but when the power plants were automated, the town site was levelled and grassed over.

Somewhere around Fraserdale a visitor makes his probably unremarked entrance into the public area of the train. The

Freighter canoe riding light and high en route to Moose Factory.

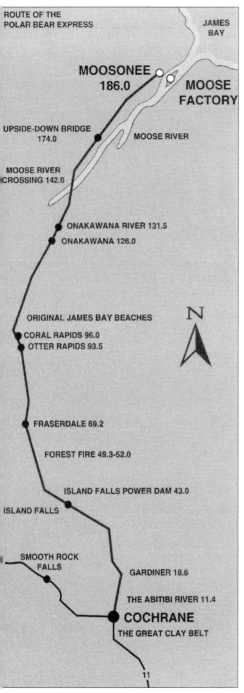

Route of the Polar Bear.

engineers take turns coming back for a meal. Fortunate travellers in the diner sometimes get a chance to chat with these veterans of the Polar Bear Express. Others may be just watching the scenery and making new friends, while those with children may locate them in the entertainment car.

Up at Otter Rapids, **mileage 93.5**, the train slows to give travellers a view of the generating station to the right of the train. This 174,800 kilowatt-capacity unit works by remote control. Defective units shut themselves down until repair crews arrive by boat, rail car, or even helicopter. In spring the excess water cascades over the spillway like a miniature Niagara Falls.

The original prehistoric beaches of James Bay are located at **mileage 94**. This is the start today of the Hudson Bay Lowlands, one of the largest wetlands in the world. This is permafrost country, a place where bog, fen and forest mix. Spagnum moss and lichens grow in the bogs while sedges predominate in the fens. The best stands of trees are seen in well drained areas along the river banks.

Inland they are stunted due to poor drainage.

Coral Rapids appears at **mileage 96.3**. The gravel pits supply some ballast for the railway. Fossil hunters enjoy the place since sharks teeth found embedded in coral prove the existence of a one-time tropical sea. A more valuable resource in the area may turn out to be kimberlite, host mineral for diamonds. Riders will note a power line on the left hand side of the train. This improvement of 1977 saw the end of

Santa reaches James Bay by the year-round Little Bear.

expensive diesel and coal power plants at the end of the line. The tall poles contrast with the generally small trees in the vicinity.

Sometimes the Little Bear meets the big Polar Bear on this section of the line. In railway jargon, the mixed freight, being third class, is inferior, while the passenger train avoids the siding because it is superior, or first class. Such passes could occur at **mileage 126**. This is home to a vast as yet untapped deposit of brown coal or lignite. There are at least two and one-half million metric tons of the soft, watery coal. The deposit has been known for 200 years.

From Fraserdale north the train takes on a more pronounced roll. This is because the ride is harder on sand; south of the big hydro development, the rock ballast underlying the tracks all the way to Cochrane offers a far smoother ride. Periodically the engineer drops his speed because it helps the dining car attendants serve dishes like soup.

Blue herons may often be seen in the vicinity of Onakawana River, **mileage 131.5**. This river is a good fishing area, along with companion waterways, the Otakwahegan, **mileage 158**, and the Kwataboahagen, **mileage 174**. The latter is crossed by a rarity for railway construction, an upside-down bridge. Girders on such bridges normally run under the road bed but over ice-filled rivers during spring break-up, this could cause an obstruction, so the supports are up to offer clear passage for ice chunks. Watch out for other such oddities at **mileage 176 and 180**.

As the train eases through Moose River Crossing at **mileage 142** there is little indication that this is a special location on the railway. At one time there was even a small village here with its own school. The bridge itself is 549 metres long, a $1,000,000 engineering triumph in Depression years. The train slows to make the 800-metre long crossing. In summer the river is sluggish but in spring the ice-filled torrent is a potential problem for bridge supports; on occasion dynamite has been used to break up ice jams. Watch out for small white caps in the waters below. These rapids remind us of hard going for fur trade canoes years ago.

The last few miles seem to flash by. Renison, **mileage 156**, honours the tough Anglican Bishop of Moosonee who greeted early railway builders in 1908 by snowshoeing to Cochrane. At Cheepash River, **mileage 162**, there are huge gypsum deposits under the ever-present bush but the only sign of human presence is a lone sectionman's house.

The water tower, **mileage 186**, gives the first glimpse of Moosonee. Most visitors head off at once to see the sights of the land at the end of the line, but those who visit the station could see a "gold" spike and hammer placed there to commemorate the fortieth anniversary of the completion of construction. The station looks rather utilitarian, yet it is considered worth preserving as the sole survivor in the country of this particular building style.

Travellers on the return trip have had their fill of touring and relax, visit the entertainment car or enjoy a meal. Company representatives are anxious to gauge passengers' opinions about the excursion with a view to service improvement, so a survey form is offered so that the line may respond to riders' needs.

As travellers return to Cochrane, they might consider the zigzag lines which appear on the Ontario government railway equipment. Think of them as tire treads and rail tracks, even electronic communications which link this lonely land served by the Ontario Northland and improve the lives of its year-round residents. Riders who have been down north on the Polar Bear Express have good and lasting memories of their ride and the country at the end of the line.

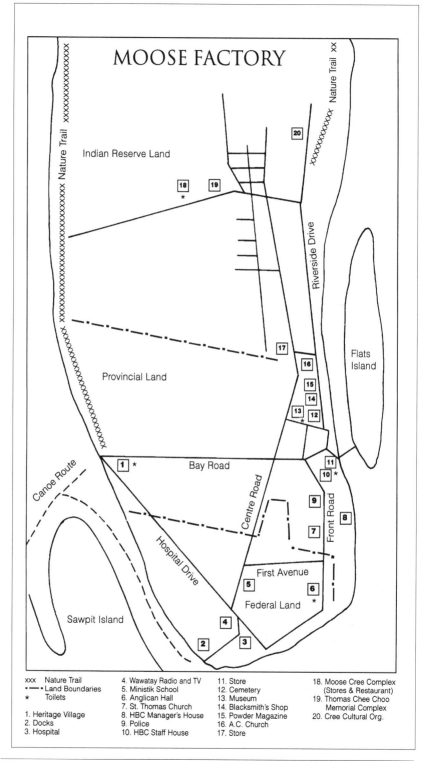

MOOSE FACTORY

Indian Reserve Land

Nature Trail xxx

Nature Trail xx

20

18 19
★

Riverside Drive

Provincial Land

17

16

15

14

13 12
★

Flats Island

Canoe Route

1 ★

Bay Road

11
10 ★

9

Centre Road

Front Road

8

7

Hospital Drive

First Avenue

5

6
★

Federal Land

Sawpit Island

4

2 3

xxx   Nature Trail
•—•—• Land Boundaries
★   Toilets

1. Heritage Village
2. Docks
3. Hospital

4. Wawatay Radio and TV
5. Ministik School
6. Anglican Hall
7. St. Thomas Church
8. HBC Manager's House
9. Police
10. HBC Staff House

11. Store
12. Cemetery
13. Museum
14. Blacksmith's Shop
15. Powder Magazine
16. A.C. Church
17. Store

18. Moose Cree Complex
    (Stores & Restaurant)
19. Thomas Chee Choo
    Memorial Complex
20. Cree Cultural Org.

5

Life at the Bottom of the Bay

THE two settlements at the bottom of James Bay are the largest in Ontario without access to the provincial highway network, even though the area is governed by the Highway Traffic Act. The whole James Bay Lowlands have a population density of 0.9 to the square kilometre.

Climate gives a fair idea of the place. There is less sun than in southern centres, but in July as many as 225 hours of the warming rays shine on the Moose estuary. By contrast, at ninety millimeters, more rain is received in the area than falls on major southern centres. There is less snow compared to the accumulations experienced by Timmins, Toronto and Thunder Bay but there are fierce Arctic gales and bitter wind chill factors.

Nature rules in this part of the world. In summer the land is a blend of greens standing out among the great confusion of lakes, rivers and swamps. The white of winter serves to etch out the trees and define the swamps, the rivers snaking north, the cut-off curls of oxbow lakes and the thousands of waters which have no name. Among all this only man brings the straight line. Hydro poles and steel tracks stand out in the landscape in angular symmetry.

Most visitors spend a short period at Moosonee and Moose Factory. To really know what life is like in this still-lonely land, one must live there through the seasons. Here is just a glimpse of times when the tourist influx is over for another year.

This scene could have been taken today, instead it was captured in 1932.

Sunset on the flats near Hannah Bay goose camp.

The character of these communities is shaped by location, but in many ways life proceeds as it does anywhere else. Advertising in *The Freighter* indicates amenities available to ordinary people that were not enjoyed even thirty years ago. There is a wide range of local goods and services, and merchants in Timmins and Cochrane actively court the patronage of residents. Eight churches offer services and these are well attended. There are service clubs and youth organizations such as Scouts and Guides. One popular new interest is a chapter of Ducks Unlimited. Ducks certainly are unlimited in this part of the world, and the support for this group is an indication of the generosity of the people of the area in working for the benefit of people outside the region.

Isolation is a relative term. The delta area receives CBC radio and cable television as well as local radio and television. The Chamber of Commerce has supported such initiatives since communications opportunities were first presented. Other accomplishments of this body include airport upgrading, work on civic improvements and the maintenance of the Moose River navigation system. People willing to give freely of their time abound in this place. There are volunteer fire departments and the meals on wheels programme is well supported.

The Moosonee Development Area Board, a seven-member body appointed by the province, is somewhat similar to a municipal council except that it has jurisdiction over 400 square miles. The board is responsible for the airport, public works, recreation, a family resource centre and the fire department.

Historic St. Thomas Anglican Church, early Anglican Cathedral Church of the Cree.

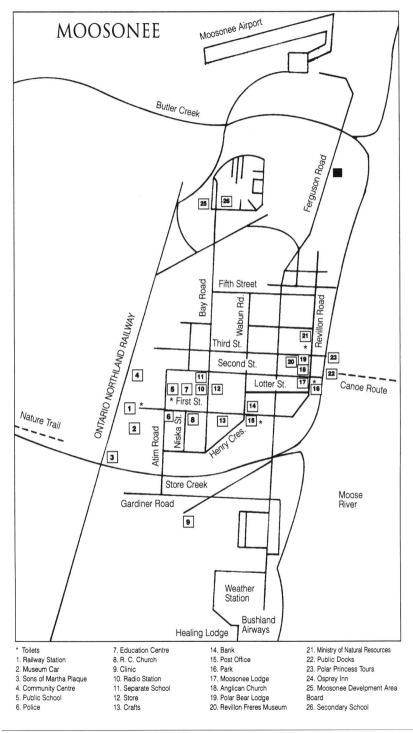

MOOSONEE

Moosonee Airport

Butler Creek

Ferguson Road

Bay Road

Fifth Street

Wabun Rd.

Revillon Road

ONTARIO NORTHLAND RAILWAY

Third St.

Second St.

Lotter St.

Canoe Route

First St.

Nature Trail

Atim Road

Niska St.

Henry Cres.

Store Creek

Gardiner Road

Moose River

Weather Station

Bushland Airways

Healing Lodge

25 26

21 *

20 19
    18

23

22

17 *
16

11

4

5 7 10 12

1 *

14

6

8 13 15 *

2

3

9

* Toilets
1. Railway Station
2. Museum Car
3. Sons of Martha Plaque
4. Community Centre
5. Public School
6. Police

7. Education Centre
8. R. C. Church
9. Clinic
10. Radio Station
11. Separate School
12. Store
13. Crafts

14. Bank
15. Post Office
16. Park
17. Moosonee Lodge
18. Anglican Church
19. Polar Bear Lodge
20. Revillon Freres Museum

21. Ministry of Natural Resources
22. Public Docks
23. Polar Princess Tours
24. Osprey Inn
25. Moosonee Develpment Area Board
26. Secondary School

The Moosonee Logo, in Cree and English, is most distinctive.

The student-designed school crest shows its namesake Aurora Borealis

Current work for the board includes expansion of sewage treatment facilities and bridge construction. The organization provides community infrastructure for the mainland town of around 2,000 people.

Moose Factory is a more complex place to administer. The island has federal and provincial lands as well as the Moose Cree Band reserve.

One service subject to seasonal fluctuation is the mail. In freeze-up and break-up on the Moose River, the post comes over by helicopter. Groceries are brought by air lift at these times.

The big employer on the island is the hospital. The majority of workers there come from Moose Factory. The facility serves a wide area and several James Bay communities rely on its services.

The RCMP no longer work on the big island and even the provincial police have given way to Cree police officers. The OPP and the Nishnawbe Police Service work in close harmony. The distinguishing badge of the island police is not really representative of local culture, as it is a thunderbird, an emblem with more west coast significance. The incidents handled by these officers are much the same as anywhere else but there is a local flavour. Officers tend to spend time counselling and adapt their policing to traditional ways. Both police services unite in looking out for citizens' welfare. In winter this can include keeping a weather eye out for people wandering in severe cold temperatures. As for the OPP, the posting to Moosonee remains popular and officers often opt to extend their tour of duty there.

Education is a major preoccupation of northern people. Opportunities for children have vastly improved over the past quarter century. Elementary education is offered on the mainland and on Moose Factory. Teachers from the south would note some

At dusk the boat taxi man anchors his boat for the night.

differences in the curriculum and school year. Helicopter, boating and ice travel safety are common school topics. The school year is adjusted so that children may accompany their parents on the annual goose hunt. Safe hunting courses are followed by experience bagging geese. Instructors teach the Cree language and children learn the ways of their people. Many will have a distinct advantage in later life as they have the opportunity to become fluent in Cree, French and English.

The founding of the Northern Lights Secondary School on the site of the former radar base to the north of Moosonee means that adolescents no longer have to leave their home area to receive high school experiences appropriate to their needs. The school crest, with the stylized northern lights dancing over the forest green, is often seen beyond the confines of the area. Students now often go out to sports events, conferences and academic functions across the province. Senior students have participated in exchange programmes with other countries. Recently a group participated in the North American Indigenous Games in Minnesota.

With public education entrenched in a continuous stream in the area, it follows that adult education is a priority for upgrading and work-related needs. While students go out to university, JBEC, the James Bay Education Centre, a campus of Northern College of Applied Arts and Technology, offers a variety of courses especially tailored to aboriginal needs. Showcases in the foyer of this institution depict local skills, crafts and trades. The library and daycare service are well patronized.

The Ministry of Natural Resources has a strong presence in the area. The largest in Ontario, Moosonee District covers more than 200,000 square kilometres, one-fifth of the land area of the province. Information provided by this agency is most helpful, including such advice as that freeze-up occurs around November 12th, and spring break-up of the river ice takes place anywhere between April 18th and May 12th. The MNR is responsible for bird sanctuaries, wetlands of international importance. The economic spinoff from hunting is enormous, as more than 80,000 geese are taken annually. Hunt camps bring in needed employment dollars. Trappers also add to the area's economy, not only taking fur for sale on international markets but also for use in regional crafts.

Apart from museum connections, the organization which brought the first Europeans to the north and fought the French to keep its monopoly is long gone from the lowlands. The Hudson Bay Company pulled out of the retail store business in the north and its network was taken over by a retail newcomer. Now called the North West Company, they operate Northern stores and a tour of the two outlets in the area gives a good idea of products required along the river.

Recreation is a big part of life at Moosonee and Moose Factory. Both locations have modern arenas and every sport imaginable is in vogue, with the predictable exception of downhill skiing. Area teams compete around the north. People make their own amusements; in summer everyone uses the river and in snow months the snowmobile is heard everywhere. River watching may

The big Ministik School is quiet before children make their way to classes.

be the activity least mentioned, yet it is a constant source of entertainment. The great Moose River is always a study in activity and colour. The grinding rush of great chunks of ice, several tons in weight and up to fifteen metres high, is a magnificent sight in the spring break-up time. Rain, wind and fog add a new dimension to travel on the river for much of the year. In winter, a white-out coming down from the Bay can send travellers scurrying for the haven of lighted streets. In mid-February the annual Cree Winter Games or Keematowan offers family fun from dog racing to individual and group activities. The best time to watch the Aurora Borealis, the spectacular light show of the northern lights, is in fall or spring.

In the light. The old St.Thomas Church has survived ice and flood for more than 150 years.

PAUL MCLEOD

Employment is a major concern for those who live in the area. There is never enough to go around. For the most part, jobs are provided by the railways, air travel, government, tourism and related service industries. Much of the work is seasonal, such as during the excursion train period, goose hunt season and with shipping and freight forwarding firms. Cottage industries have developed to manufacture and sell area crafts. Moose hide mitts, boots and slippers sell well. Tamarack and other decoys are in demand as decorator gifts. Printmaking, sculpture and painting are generally well done and local pieces sell across the continent.

Life at the bottom of the Bay is continually changing and adapting to current needs. Nothing is constant in the lowlands except change.

6

First People of the Lowlands

Our destiny is not a place, it is the true and lasting good
of man in this region.

*Ka ishtichiyak mona itawiniwan ekawanima kakik
keishiminotanin pan ininiw ota a skik.*

ᑲ ᐃᓐᑎᒋᐳ ᒍᐊ ᐃᑕᐧᐃᓂᐧᐊᑉ ᐁᐧᑲᓄᒪ ᑲᑭ
ᕿᐃᔑᒥᓄᑕᓄᐸᐧᑉ ᐃᓂᓂ ᐅᑕ ᐊᑭᐸᕻ

THE Cree are the largest Indian group in Canada, living in an arc from Alberta running through to Quebec. Their native tongue is a branch of the Algonkian family of languages. There are the Plains Cree, the Woods Cree and the people around James Bay, the Swampy Cree. Actually the word Cree is normally only used in writing; they traditionally refer to themselves as "the people," and more recently according to the names of political groups which represent their views.

Moosonee has no Indian band. The town population is about 2,000, of which perhaps 1,800 are native, having come from other James Bay communities during the period since the railway first arrived on the Moose River or born to these original migrants. Moose Factory has the larger population of the two communities, with about 2,300 people, about 1,500 from the Moose Band, 400 from Mocreebec, who came originally from Quebec, 200 who live

Gathering moss, 1923.

C 20851

PA 99583

All decked out in Sunday best at Moose Factory, 1926.

off the reserve and about 200 non-natives. Whereas the mainland is administered by the Moosonee Development Area Board, the island is federal land at the south end, home of most non-natives, the centre is provincial land, home to many of the Mocreebec residents and the larger, northern portion is the location of the Moose Band reserve.

There are two other groups, which represent all First Nations people. The Mushikegowuk (People of the Swamps) Council is a federation of all six bands, represented by their chiefs, on western

Trapper, circa 1940.

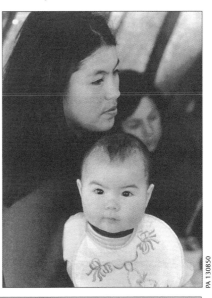

Mother and child, 1973.

Teenage boys being taken out on the river to learn the old ways from Cree instructors Bert Jeffries (front) and Jack Smallboy (steering the freighter canoe), spring, 1995.

James Bay. Employees of this group monitor government activity, analyze policy, and look out for the social, educational and economic welfare of their people. Treaty Nine is the agreement with the federal government which covers most of Northern Ontario. Now the Ojibway have joined with the Cree to form Nishnawbe-Aski, an alliance which covers the old treaty area, and deals directly with government.

Wayne Tomatuk, a good artist and a proficient steersman on the Moose River.

PAUL McLEOD

Acceptance as an Indian person is important. A status Indian is one entered on band council rolls and eligible to receive the benefits arising from membership. Those outside a band are referred to as non-status. The band makes decisions on housing, welfare, local services and employment. The last three decades have seen a growth in First Nations services. There is Keewaytinok,

PA 130851

Craft work in a meshewup or tipi, 1973. Today visitors are more likley to see bannock made in the tipi.

PA 130639

Drying hides,1980. Today the substandard housing in background once used at Moose Factory by people arriving from Quebec is long gone.

PAUL McLEOD

Girls out on school trip, spring 1995, learn fishing as part of the old ways.

PAUL McLEOD

The photographer's mother, Stella McLeod, roasting a goose over an open fire, spring, 1995.

the legal service. Puyukotayno is the Cree equivalent of the Children's Aid. The Band places much importance on the maintenance of the Cree language, and children are taught traditional ways, including living out on the land.

Visitors will note a host of organizations catering to Cree needs and interests. Not long ago there was little opportunity for Indian entrepreneurs to go into business as it was difficult to obtain start-up loans. Now there are several means available for budding business people to get a loan to build their enterprise. Impressive among the business ventures which have commenced in the last few years are those sponsored by the Mocreebec. The people who came from Quebec had no land when they arrived. When the author lived on the island in the sixties, the newcomers lived in tents year-round. In recent years they have obtained land, built houses and begun to prosper. They have their own chief and council now. Some of their endeavours include non-profit housing, a restaurant, bakery, craft shop, and the cable-television system for both the island and mainland.

Newcomers will see problems similar to their own home towns when they visit Moosonee and Moose Factory. There is unemployment and there are social problems. But the newcomer will notice the growing empowerment of the Cree people. Instead of being led by non-natives and having decisions made for them by government far removed from the Moose River area, they are now taking charge of their own destiny and running Cree affairs, from business through to education. Graduates of technical and professional courses return to take leadership roles. In traditional native spiritual practice, the two traditional church affiliations are challenged by evangelical and other charismatic faiths. In these as in other interests, the First Nations people have choices now and they pursue new opportunities.

Since the time when the Hudson Bay Company first came to James Bay, the Cree have adapted to change and profited from it. The time of the Cree has come. They are taking their rightful place as leaders in the stewardship of the Hudson Bay Lowlands. We conclude with a statement which sums up their feelings:

> In this land, no achievement by any people is real unless it respects those who are its First People.

> *Ota askik mona itakawan kashkiowin piko keko awenikanak mona wayesh ikin tanetotakik mona wayesh ina pataniniw eki ekishtenichika tenik anikinishew ininiwak.*

> ᐅᑕ ᐊᔨᑭᐢ ᒧᓇ ᐃᑕᑲᐧᐊᐣ ᑲᔥᐱᐅᐧᐃᐣ ᐱᑯ ᑫᑯ ᐊᐧᐁᕓᓄᐸᐦᐠ ᒧᓇ ᐧᐊᔦᔲ ᐊᐱᐣ ᑕᓄᐧᑕᑲᐠᐢ ᒧᓇ ᐧᐊᔦᔲ ᐊᓇᐸᐟᐊᓄᕞᐤ ᐁᐱ ᐱᓄᐅᕓᑳᐧᐅᕓᐢ ᐊᐧᓄᐸᐧᑥᐢᐤ ᐊᕓᕓᐧᐊᐢ.

Hunting partner on Horseshoe Island, Moose River estuary.

This Cree-owned Air Creebec aircraft awaits passengers at the new Moosonee airport terminal.

7

By Air with the Cree

TRADITIONALLY tourists visit Moosonee and Moose Factory via the excursion train. But there is another way to access the bottom of James Bay used by locals and those on business who wish to arrive in less than a quarter of the time taken by the train. Visitors can fly to the communities on the Moose River using an airline which a few short years after its founding is held up as a model First Nations success story.

In 1975 the Grand Council of the Cree of Quebec took political control of their land, economic development and social services from the federal government on behalf of their far-flung people. The man who led the way in this visionary move was Grand Chief Billy Diamond. The charismatic Cree leader called Rupert's House home, but parlayed the new-found clout of his people into board rooms and government offices across the continent and abroad.

The veteran native politician and his advisers searched for ways of investing native funds so that the First Nations people might increase their capital base. There was no difficulty identifying the first major target for expansion. There are few roads in the vast region around James and Hudson Bays and air travel is the most common way to go. There was a ready market among the Cree, government and business people, and also the promise of tourist travel.

The pioneer airline of the area for half a century was Austin Airlines. Principal owners, the De Luce family, were interested in selling their company, and as a result Air Creebec was born in 1980, using as its base the assets of the Austin group. Within eight years all outstanding shares in the operation had been purchased by its new owners for $19.4 million. This made Air Creebec a totally Cree-owned business; the deal was the largest commercial transaction made by any native group in Canada to that date.

The new star in the commercial airline skies grew from thirty employees in 1986 to 180 in 1995. There were growing pains and problems maintaining service over a vast area and ensuring a healthy bottom line, but the Cree enterprise won its wings. Apart from scheduled operations the firm branched into profitable charter agreements. These included federal and provincial ministry work, retail and resource-based private enterprise contract flying and supply services for big utilities, such as the James Bay hydro project. People in communities along James Bay sometimes charter aircraft

Passengers board the big Hawker-Siddeley 748 aircraft. This machine is configured for passengers in the rear and freight forward. The distinctive Air Creebec logo features the geese of the lowlands.

to pay their respects at funerals of respected residents in another village. In a lighter vein, they book aircraft to attend fund-raising bingos held by their neighbours. The airline puts on special charters for Christmas shoppers and also for goose hunters in season.

Since 1987 the northern airline has picked up a host of awards including some originating with the province of Quebec, such as Company of the Year in 1990, Imperial Oil and other private company service accolades. The best recognition is always from the home ground and in 1995 the airline took home the Business of the Year award among northern Ontario businesses.

Air Creebec has scheduled flights to connect with its northern network out of Montreal, but the three main bases are Timmins, Moosonee and Val d'Or. Timmins is the centre for Ontario operations and Val d'Or serves Quebec. Out of Timmins in its western swing the airline serves Cochrane, Moosonee, Fort Albany, Kashechewan, Attawapiskat and Peawanuk. Eastern links via the Val d'Or hub are Waskaganish, Eastmain, Wmindji and Chisasibi. On the way north from Montreal stops are made at Chibougamau and Nemaska. Flights also serve the great hydro complexes of northern Quebec.

Air Creebec connects with its computerized reservations system to regional, provincial, national and world-wide air services. It is an Air Canada feeder line. All this added up to 100,000 passengers, twelve million pounds of freight carried and revenue of roughly $30 million in 1995. With Beech 1900D, Hawker-Siddley 748 and two types of the Dash 8 aircraft, the line can offer seating varying from nineteen to fifty passengers and cargo varying from 650 to 15,000 pounds.

Current Air Creebec president is Albert Diamond. This long-time Cree entrepreneur formerly ran a native construction company, boosting revenues from $3 to $64 million for the 12,000-plus Cree of northern Quebec. He is no politician like his brother Billy; he is a businessman. Albert smiles when he recalls the early days of travel in the region. "Before," he says, "air travel cost an arm and a leg. He shrugs. Under careful stewardship the Cree can now move easily in their area at a reasonable cost and make money for their people at the same time.

Passengers flying via Air Creebec arriving or departing from the bright 1991 Moosonee airport terminal may well be served by Cree aircrew. The Moose Cree First Nation has sponsored young flyers, and the confidence shown in them has gone far to produce success in aviation. Moose Factory band member Russell Hunter flies both charter and scheduled flights. Terry McLeod, also from the big island, is a captain on the Dash 8 aircraft.

A typical hour-long scheduled flight to Moosonee from Timmins may carry Cree pilot Terry McLeod as captain, Ray Christman in the right hand seat and Dorothy Lemieux working as flight attendant. From Timmins north the Dash 8-100 series aircraft flies over a skein of waterways fringed by northern swamps and evergreens. From the 16,000 feet cruising altitude, the pilots know they are following routes pioneered by trappers and fur traders three hundred years ago. All Air Creebec flight crew are veterans of thousands of hours flying in the region, but the changing face of the land never fails to interest the pilots between their busy work and safety-check schedules.

ONTARIO TOURISM

Even though there are no Polar Bears in the Clay Belt, Chimo has become the symbol of Cochrane, home of the famed train.

8

Making the Most of Touring Time

A LL vacations have a cost in terms of time and money, and visitors to the land north of Cochrane will want to make the most of their trip by planning well ahead of time. In the section at the rear of the book on Helpful Facts, the addresses of all necessary information sources are given.

There are four sets of touring suggestions for the first-time visitor. These are:

- The Northern Corridor: North Bay to Cochrane
- Cochrane and area
- Moose Factory
- Moosonee

The Northern Corridor: North Bay to Cochrane

These suggestions will take the visitor north. Just reverse them if you intend to catch up on them on the way south.

Temagami, about an hour north of North Bay, is set in a great pine forest. The small portion of the great lake seen from the highway is a delight, always busy with float planes and motor boats in summer. This is a gateway to a vast skein of lakes and once was the home of white-man-turned-Indian, Grey Owl. There are artifacts relating to him in Finlayson Park at the south end of town and also in the welcome centre just behind the Shell station on the left of the highway.

Latchford is a little place that capitalizes on its location; it refers to itself as "the best little town by a dam site." Check at the information hut to find out about the trip on the Montreal River by voyageur canoe. Visit the museum, the House of Memories and see early days of lumbering in the Loggers' Hall of Fame.

On the left of the highway just before the Cobalt bypass is a large frame building, the Highway Book Shop. It has probably the largest collection of books under one roof in the north country. It is a delight to explore the rambling building finding books old and new as well as its own extensive list of publications.

A trip off the main highway to Cobalt is highly recommended. With its switch-back streets and rugged terrain the silver town is unique in Canada. Take in the mining museum and pick up a pamphlet for the self-guided silver tour around long-gone mine sites. The former railway station is now a military museum, The

The venerable St. Thomas Anglican Church, Moose Factory.

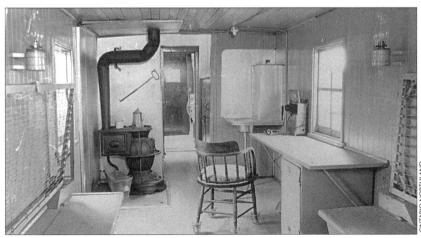

Inside the caboose of Cochrane's Railway Museum.

Bilingual memorial – Cree and English – to Bishop Horden, first Bishop of Moosonee.

Bunker. Before you leave the silver town, take a picture of the one-time store built around a mine head frame near the museum, which now houses a northern publishing firm, *The Highgrader* magazine. Now you can return to the highway or keep on the bypass to Haileybury. Attractions here are the large waterfront swimming and boating complex, the Fire Museum close by Lake Timiskaming and the art gallery in the public library which you pass on your way north out of town.

New Liskeard is a pretty clay belt town at the head of Lake Timiskaming with a fine waterfront, head of the waterway which may be navigated all way north from the lower Ottawa Valley. Further north of Earlton watch out for the big steel sculpture of a buffalo, announcing a large zoo. Beyond this, Englehart has an interesting museum and former steam railway engine adjacent to its modern station.

Kirkland Lake is worth a diversion from the main highway. On the way into town, the striking white building across from the

Summer soldiers dressed in the uniform of the De Troyes era fire their muskets at Moose Factory.

Hudson Bay Company and Anglican flags flank the Bishop's window, St. Thomas Church, Moose Factory. Note the barrel- or boat-shaped roof.

The chancel and choir stalls, St. Thomas Church. In summer the precious moose hide altar cloths are dsplayed.

The old Hudson Bay Company graveyard, Moose Factory. Some of the board markers have letters incised with lead.

The inscriptions on the old Moose Factory graveyard are a must-read for visitors. The schooner Nouveau Quebec is in the background.

Comfort Inn is a funeral home housed in former mine buildings. Just beyond, on the same side, is the Museum of Northern History, once the Chateau, home of Sir Harry Oakes, famous gold mining magnate. The town built on "the mile of gold" has much to see and is on the route to Quebec.

Matheson has a fine museum off to the left of the highway. The Thelma Miles Museum ingeniously crams a great deal of local memorabilia into a small place. One more stop might be at Iroquois Falls to take the woodlands and pulp and paper tour. Then it is off to Cochrane and the way north on the Polar Bear Express.

Cochrane – The Polar Bear Town

The area along the railway tracks in Cochrane is, well, industrial. There is little worthy of attention there except the museum in an old train on an adjacent siding. But just a couple of minutes across Railway Street past the railway museum, Commando Lake is well worth a visit. It is a good spot for a walk or a picnic. Not many towns have such a nice waterway in the middle of the community, and since no power boats are allowed, the beach on the north side is great for swimming.

The Information Hut at the entrance to town by the statue of Chimo the Polar Bear is a handy place to pick up brochures. Ask about the opportunity to be up close to the polar bears at the new Polar Bear Habitat on Drury Road, not far from the train station.

Cochrane was laid out by the railway in 1908 and so it has broad streets, especially in the main business area, Sixth Street, which is a block west of the station. The older portion of town is mainly the blocks around the lakes. Newer homes are to the north. The District Office of the Ministry of Natural Resources, close by the Information Hut, has all sorts of information on canoe routes, fishing areas and provincial parks. Not far away on Fourth Street is the elegant courthouse for the Cochrane District. In the south they have counties; here in the north areas are so vast and people so few that the administrative units are districts, many times the size of southern counties. Timmins is a city in the district but Cochrane, with less than 5,000 people, is the district town.

Few people can be unaware of Tim Horton, the hockey player who spawned a chain of coffee shops. Horton came from Cochrane and the arena on Third Avenue is named for him. The town he left long ago boasts one of the longest-running and certainly the most northerly fall fairs in the province. In winter they have a great carnival on Lake Commando, where hardy souls jump through the ice in the Polar Bear Dip. The whole area is hooked into a vast network of snowmobile trails. Generally, visitors stay at one of the motels along the entrance to town on Highway 11, but some go further west to accommodations at a small village called Hunta.

By far the most visitors to James Bay come via the Polar Bear Express. It is suggested that they see Moose Factory as the oldest

The tour dock at Moosonee is first stop on trips out to James Bay.

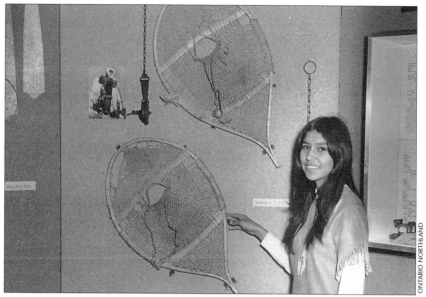

Emily Faries displays exhibits at the Moose Factory Museum.

community first, and then explore Moosonee on their return. This allows maximum benefit from the four and a half hours the excursion train provides. Those who come up on one train and return south on another have more options and flexibility in exploring the area. Excursion travellers should head straight down First Street to the docks shown on the Moosonee map. The freighter canoes have a set one-way price and are just like taxis. Boatmen will call out and invite passengers aboard.

Some words of caution: visitors to these northern communities are guests of the people who live there. They are busy places and not museums. Be considerate. If you wish to take pictures of these, your hosts, please be courteous and ask first.

Moose Factory – Ontario's oldest settlement

The canoe trip to Moose Factory – the oldest settlement in Ontario, founded in 1672 – is roughly 3.2 kilometres. After the canoe passes Tidewater Provincial Park on Charles Island it runs by Sawpit Island, so named for the early times when logs were sawn by hand, one man in a pit below, the other above. On the shoreline, note the occasional uprooted tree and gouges in the bank. This natural sculpture is done by rampaging ice in spring break-up time.

When the canoe docks, follow the map and take the route to your right. This winds along the east side of the island and will give you an opportunity to see the historic features. The rest of the sightseeing can come later. Just budget perhaps ten minutes for the return trip and up to ten minutes for possible waiting time. Check the map for the locations of toilets. This is handy information which will give new meaning to the term comfort station.

Old cannons at Moose Factory, formerly used to greet the arrival of important persons or announce great events.

Part of the route past the 126-bed Weeneebaykon (formerly Moose Factory General Hospital) is on a dike built to protect the shoreline from erosion. In this area there are hydro poles pile-driven into the bank to underpin the dike. The three-storey building is built in the shape of the Cross of Lorraine, symbol of the scourge of tuberculosis which was once a focus of treatment here. The hospital has been serving the lower James Bay area since 1950 and has a heliport for fly-in cases. Houses just north of the hospital are for

The waterfront pavilion at Moosonee is a good place for lunch or to watch the ever-changing river.

The blacksmith's shop at Moose factory is one of three buildings remaining from the fur trade past. Note the ship's capstan.

doctors and other medical staff. Note the overhead pipes which heat these homes from the hospital plant. Along the way note what appear to be tipis. In actual fact they are a way of storing poles for firewood, arranged so that rain and snow slide off easily. The big building just off First Avenue is Ministik School, provider of education up to grade eight on the island. When the author was supervising principal on the island in the mid-sixties there were four schools, but now they are consolidated into this building. There was also a residential school nearby but children no longer come to school here from up the coast. Instead they receive their education in their own communities.

The Anglican Parish Hall is a nice spot to relax, buy native crafts like the tamarack twig decoys with their pleasant aroma, take tea or coffee or just relax and look at the displays. The Anglican Church Women support their church by this means. Look out for Cree hymn books, calendars and postcards.

Just ahead is the historic St. Thomas Church. Enter it reverently,

Once Revillon Frères, predecessor of the famous Revlon cosmetics firm, had many buildings at Moosonee. This picture dates from 1927 and the present museum is the only one left.

for this is God's house, spiritual home to many of the Cree and once their cathedral church. Pegs in the floor were placed there years ago to assist in drainage in times of flooding. The structure is made of squared logs covered with siding. The interior roof is barrel-shaped, reminiscent of the hull of a ship. There are interesting monuments, fine stained glass which came here by sea from England. See the crest of

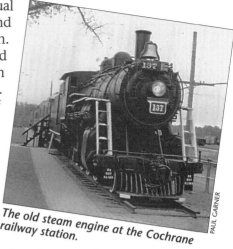

The old steam engine at the Cochrane railway station.

the Diocese of Moosonee in the south window, an island with the sun above and a canoe. The beautiful moose hide and beadwork altar cloths are fragile and should not be touched. Sit in one of the pews for a moment and look at the Cree hymn books and testaments. The Hudson Bay Company flag honours the early carpenters who built the church at a total cost of one thousand pounds. Don't forget to leave a thank-offering in the collection box on your way out to assist in building maintenance. There are many simple wood markers in the church yard but some may be incorrectly placed. Some years ago a youth hired to cut the grass uprooted several posts to make the cutting easier. He may not have replaced them all in the same spots.

Dancing the way on the return trip in the entertainment car of the Polar Bear Express.

ONTARIO NORTHLAND

Summer visitors will have several opportunities to obtain Cree crafts like those sold by this young entrepreneur.

Close by the church is a building that was once the office of the RCMP, the Ontario Provincial Police and now houses the Nishnawbe-Aski police service. A narrow passage-way passes the former Hudson Bay Company manager's house. To the left is the company staff house, the only building left of the complex that in bygone years made up the trading post. This building, built to house senior staff, visiting ship captains and other notables, was constructed to last; it has a huge foundation of bricks, lime and stone weighing fifty tons. You may see ongoing archeological work here and should visit the interpretive display mounted in the house, an impressive building with a stark, simplistic link to the eighteenth century, although it dates from 1847. The old cannons make a good photo opportunity. Next to them, the old fur press recalls a time when thousands of

PAUL McLEOD

A boat taxi heads away from the Moose Factory Cree Village Restaurant and Craft Shop. In winter this is the spot where the ice road connects with the island.

prime pelts were shipped from this land, pressed and bailed here for ease of shipment by sea to European markets. Beyond are the tidal flats. Once there was a bell tower here, scores of buildings and schooners pulled up on the shores.

Centennial Park has a small museum; the Blacksmith's Shop, built in 1740 is probably the oldest wooden building in Ontario. The fragile state of the old powder magazine nearby does not permit entry. Here powder and shot for ship and land-based guns was stored as well as musket ball and powder.

Water taxi boatmen of the new generation decorate their freighter canoes in imaginative ways.

Beyond is the old graveyard. The markers here are made of pine, stone and marble and are similar to eighteenth century New England and English cemeteries. Some were incised with lead to preserve their form. Many were carved elsewhere, which accounts for the spelling errors on some, like "Moore" Factory. Evidence of epidemics of the first part of the nineteenth century is seen in numerous graves of children aged one to four years. Life was hard then, without the

A study in contrasts; tipi next to a dish antenna.

benefit of the variety of medicines enjoyed today. The cemetery is much more extensive than it appears and from time to time more graves are located.

The markers tell their own story. Mary Thomas was born in 1791 and died when lost on the ice in 1802 with an Indian family. The Anglican prayer book is echoed in the inscription, "From sudden death, Good Lord deliver us." The ship's surgeon's grave marker announces that he died in 1807, at the age of 28 years, "much regretted by all who knew him."

All points on the island are within easy walking distance. Visitors could return to the docks or walk further north on Riverside Drive and visit the Cree Cultural Centre to see the handicrafts, souvenirs and exhibits there. Just a short distance west is the Thomas Cheechoo Arena and the Moose Cree Complex. This building has a Northern Store, successor to the Hudson Bay Company, the band-operated Trapper's Lodge and other stores and offices.

Walk briskly now along Centre Road and cut through the middle of the island. You may either continue to the docks or turn right at Bay Road and walk to the Cree Cultural Village. Along the way here and in Moosonee you may see children selling crafts. Any that appear like rough stones could in reality be 350-million-year-old fossils from the Devonian period. The village offers a souvenir shop, restaurant and amphitheater. If the tipi is open, sample bannock cooked on an open fire.

Moose Factory Island looking south. Note the Cross-of-Lorraine-shaped hospital.

Moosonee looking south, showing the railway station centre.

A freighter canoe may be taken from here as well as from the docks where you first arrived.

Moosonee: Head of Steel

On the way back to Moosonee, observe the river. You may see the Polar Princess tour boat, or long low barges. These vessels supply James Bay villages with fuel, building materials, vehicles and other items. Tugs may be at rest, beached on the river banks. Transport looms large in this area. In winter the role of the barges is taken over by tractor roads that move their tracks north on ice roads keeping supply lanes open. Moosonee, despite some paved streets and many modern conveniences, is still very much a frontier town and the place is accustomed to being a jumping-off spot for those travelling further north.

Some visitors in fall do not go too far, they come for the great goose hunt. There are several goose camps in Hannah Bay and vicinity. Not all arrivals are hunters; the sight of thousands of geese migrating south on their way from as far north as Baffin Island to southern hot spots like Louisiana attracts many photographers and bird watchers.

The handsome building occupied by Ontario government offices houses a courthouse at one end and the Ministry of Natural Resources facilities at the other. There is a great wildlife display and interpretive centre in the building. People working out of this office have conservation responsibilities for a large chunk of wildlife real estate.

The old-world building with the mansard roof by the Polar Bear Lodge is the only building left of the once-extensive Revillon Fur Company operation. This is one of the few remaining places that once belonged to the upstart fur traders who dared go up against the mighty Hudson Bay Company. The fur museum is well worth a visit; they even have a video of a famous movie sponsored by the company back in 1930, *On to Ungava*, the story of life at company posts. Today the Revlon fur and perfume boutiques in exclusive stores are reminders that although the company no longer trades pelts, it is still one of the world's great furriers.

On the way back up First Street toward the railway station, do visit the Roman Catholic Christ the King Cathedral. The present church dates from 1946; its splendid collection of stained glass is its major attraction. Designed by native artist Keena and fabricated by Detlief Gotzens, they were installed in 1987. See especially the Indian nativity, the snowshoe window, a rendering of Kateri-Tekakwitha, the 1656-80 Mohawk virgin beatified in 1980. Remember to leave a contribution toward church upkeep as you leave.

PAUL GARNER

Fine stained glass of the Roman Catholic Cathedral, Moosonee.

Most places of interest are on First Street on the route to the station. At the end near the river, check out the Arctic Arts log building. This is a fine spot to obtain area handicrafts. Part of the same building houses John Reuben's art gallery. His prints are highly popular. Further along on the same side is the Sky Ranch, one of the best places to eat, although the Osprey Inn has a fine restaurant a few blocks away. There is a Visitor's Centre on the left and a grocery store on the right with a catchy name, Chilly Willy's. People often buy something there just to take home a souvenir bag with the name on it. Further up the street, the large brick

James Bay Education Centre, which stands out with its bold Cree syllabics on the facade, has interesting displays of crafts and canoe building. You will see Cree syllabics everywhere in the community, including on the side of the museum offering displays of natural and cultural history located in a green railway car by the station.

Depending on the time available, visitors might walk out to see the cairn to the Sons of Martha just south of the station or even take a taxi and ride out in the other direction, north to the site of the former radar station. Today this is a residential area and home of the Northern Lights Secondary School. Beyond this area is the Moosonee Airport, always a busy transport hub. Air Creebec planes fly to northern points from this well-used airport.

9

Helpful Facts

Finding About the Region

The area covered by much of the route north is represented by an organization which has a comprehensive information package. Contact:

The Cochrane-Timiskaming Travel Association
Bag 920
Schumacher, ON P0N 1G0
Tel. (800) 461 3766

The province of Ontario offers travel information on the area north of Cochrane through:

The Ontario Ministry of Tourism
77 Bloor St.W., 9th Floor
Toronto, ON M7A 2R9
Tel. (416) 965-9991.

Getting There

The Ontario Northland Railway offers bus service daily from Toronto to Cochrane, and rail service on the Northlander daily except Saturdays. There is a choice of trains from Cochrane to Moosonee. The popular Polar Bear Express runs every day except Friday from the end of June to Labour Day weekend in September.

The Big Bear, as locals know it, enables travellers to visit the bottom of James Bay, but only for a brief stay at the head of steel. There is also the Little Bear, carrying both passengers and freight, which runs north Tuesdays and Thursdays and returns south Wednesdays and Fridays. All train services have meal facilities.

The Ontario road network is well maintained; the only trip from the south may be made on Highway 11. Drive north from Toronto on Highway 400 which turns into Highway 11. The road takes a right turn at North Bay, some four hours driving later, and Cochrane is about four hours further on from North Bay. When prospective visitors consider travelling north to James Bay, they should reserve accommodation in Cochrane and in Moosonee if they intend to stay overnight.

Some Contact Numbers and Addresses

Ontario Northland Rail Services at Union Station in Toronto will give information about fares and train times and overnight packages offered to Moosonee.

The address is: 65 Front St.W.
Toronto, ON
Canada M5J 1E6
(416) 314-3750 or (800) 268-9281

Ontario Northland Head Office in North Bay, Ontario can be reached at: (705) 472-4500 or (800) 663-7512

There are six hotels/motels in the Cochrane area and at least two bed and breakfast spots. Vehicles may be parked free adjacent to the station.

Cochrane Station Inn (23 rooms)
200 Station Road
Cochrane, ON P0L 1C0
(705) 272-3500 or (800) 265-2356

Westway Motel (40 rooms)
Box 370
Cochrane, ON P0L 1C0
(705) 272-4285

Northern Lites Motel (38 rooms)
Box 1720
Cochrane, ON P0L 1C0
(705) 272-4281

Motel Chimo (17 rooms)
Box 2326
Cochrane, ON P0L 1C0
(705) 272-6555

Motel Cochrane (40 rooms)
Box 1, R.R.#2
Cochrane, ON P0L 1C0
(705) 272-4253

**Country Haven Bed &
Breakfast**
Hunta, ON P0L 1P0
(705) 272-6802

North Adventure Inn
Box 2640
Cochrane, ON P0L 1C0
(705) 272-6683

Long Lake Bed & Breakfast
Cochrane, ON P0L 1C0
(705) 272-6302

Tips on Ontario Northland Travel

Breakfast and lunch are available on the northbound Polar Bear and hot meals are served on the southbound run. Snacks may be purchased in transit and there is a bar car.

Dress in this part of the world is casual. Wear comfortable walking shoes, a sweater and rainwear. Insect repellent can be helpful in the early part of the summer season to combat blackflies. Only two items of baggage are permitted on the train and these have to be stowed on the overhead racks or between the seats. There is no porter service on this trip. Some items that might

This sketch is not of Moose Cree but of others in Manitoba, but the syllabics of James Evans, pictured here, are used on James Bay still.

be handy on the trip are a plastic raincoat, sweater, reading material, camera and perhaps binoculars.

Moosonee and Moose Factory Travel and Accommodation

Pay for only one-way freighter canoe travel across the Moose River to Moose Factory. There are always plenty of the big twenty-two to twenty-four foot, six-foot wide canoes. They carry lifejackets and are perfectly safe; the trip across the river, driven by boatmen who have spent their lives on the river, is a highlight of the excursion.

There are four tours available from:

Two Bay Enterprizes
Box 280, Moosonee, ON P0L 1Y0
(705) 336-2944.

These are popular and where possible should be booked ahead. There is a day trip of both communities by bus and freighter canoe which touches on the local highlights and is scheduled to get excursion travellers back to the train in time. A mini-twilight tour is available for overnight travellers. Such sleep-over visitors can also take a six-hour trip on the 100-passenger, steel-hulled Polar Princess out to the mouth of the river to see James Bay, a bird sanctuary and also tour Moose Factory. This firm has a dock-side gift shop, called the Boat House. Another trip of shorter duration goes to Fossil Island where participants can hunt for 375-million-year-old fossils and sample bannock and tea cooked on the shore.

Places to stay are:

Polar Bear Lodge (27 rooms)
Moosonee Lodge (21 rooms)
Both may be contacted at:
65 Enterprise Road
Rexdale, ON M9W 1C4
(416) 244-1495

Osprey Country Inn
Box 116, Moosonee, ON P0L 1Y0
(705) 336-2226

Cree Village Eco Lodge (20 rooms)
Box 730, Moose Factory, ON P0L 1W0
(705) 658-6400

Trapper's Lodge (14 rooms)
Box 220,
Moose Factory, ON P0L 1W0
(705) 658-4440

Tamarack Bed & Breakfast
Paul Charboneau
(705) 336-2864

Bay Road Bed & Breakfast
Barb Pappas
(705) 336-2211

CREE SYLLABICS

	ay	ei	e	o	oo	u	an	
A	▽ pay	△ pei	◺ pe	▷ po	◁ poo	◁ pu	◁ pah	•
P	∨ tay	∧ tei	∧ te	> to	> too	< tu	< tah	‹
T	∪ kay	∩ kei	∩ ke	⊃ ko	⊃ koo	⊂ ku	⊂ kah	c
K	٩ kay	ᑭ kei	ᖿ ke	ᑯ ko	ᑰ koo	ᖴ ku	ᖷ kah	ᑊ
CH	ᐟ chay	ᑊ chei	ᑊ che	ᒍ cho	ᒎ choo	ᒡ chu	ᒣ chah	ᒼ
M	┐ may	┌ mei	┌ me	┘ mo	┘ moo	L mu	L mah	ᒪ
N	᠊ᐥ nay	σ nei	σ ne	ᦖ no	ᦖ noo	ᦕ nu	ᦕ nah	ᐣ
S	↘ say	ᔭ sei	ᔅ se	ᔓ so	ᔙ soo	ᔆ su	ᔕ sah	ᔉ
SH	ᒧ shay	ᔒ shei	ᔘ she	↝ sho	↝ shoo	ᔗ shu	ᔗ shah	ᔋ
Y	ᐊ yay	ᐅ yei	ᐌ ye	ᕐ yo	ᕐ yoo	ᕁ yu	ᕄ yah	ᕀ
R	ᐴ ray	ᐢ rei	ᐟ re	ᕈ ro	ᕈ roo	ᕉ ru	ᕉ rah	ᕀ
L	ᕐ lay	ᓓ lei	ᓕ le	ᓗ lo	ᓘ loo	ᓚ lu	ᓛ lah	ᓬ
V	♥ vay	ᐱ vei	ᐱ ve	> vo	> voo	< vu	< vah	ᕝ
W	▽ way	△ wei	△ we	▷ wo	▷ woo	◁ wu	◁ wah	
X	THE CHARACTER FOR CHRIST							

Campers may wish to stay at Tidewater Provincial Park located on an island adjacent to Moose Factory.

For details contact: Park Superintendent,
                              Tidewater Provincial Park
                              Ministry of Natural Resources
                              Moosonee, ON P0L 1Y0.

See further details below.

Travelling the Little Bear

The Little Bear is the year-round train supplying and serving the northern end of the Ontario Northland system. Between Monday and Saturday travellers may go north one day and return the next. This train has meal services but none of the guides or entertainment of the excursion train. The staff can be most helpful, however, and the advantage of this ride for people like fishermen and canoeists is that it is one of the last flag stop trains in Canada. The train stops on request, anywhere.

Parks

Tidewater Provincial Park offers overnight camping for those who arrive by train, or canoeists just in from any one of the three long-distance trips down the river. Tidewater is across the river from Moosonee on Charles Island, which shields Moose Factory from the mainland. Water taxis will make the crossing to the camp grounds which offer camp sites, toilets, drinking water and picnic tables. This is a natural environment park which also hosts a Junior Ranger camp during summer months. The seventeen-year-old rangers work on improving provincial facilities.

A walk along the two-kilometre riverside trail displays lichens, the growth of sandbars in the river, white cedars, erosion caused by spring break-up ice action, and there are ostrich ferns or fiddleheads in early summer. There are chances of finding fossils of coral and marine shells dating from the time the area was covered by a shallow, warm-water sea.

The Polar Bear Provincial Park, 322 kilometres further north, is not for the faint hearted or those with shallow pockets. The trip may only be made by air to the vicinity of Cape Henrietta Maria. This is the most northerly park in Ontario. One study of the area referred to the portion near Winisk as "the ultimate in primeval, unpolluted environments, solitude and beauty." There are only four entry points to this wilderness park and Cree guides are essential. All food must be brought in and all garbage carried out.

Take care in contemplating a trip to this rugged isolated park. The land can be hard and unforgiving. This is the tundra and sub-Arctic, always breezy, and in winter, bitterly cold. Part of it is above the tree line and in summer the mosquitoes, black-, deer- and horseflies are diabolical.

Why go? Well, apart from the solitude and the great expanse of water and muskeg that seems to stretch into the sky, there are migratory birds in the thousands, and wildfowl. The name-sake polar bear frequents the area. In season see walrus, and several species of seals from the shores. There are woodland caribou, beaver, muskrats, timber wolves, arctic and red foxes, black bears, ermine, marten, fisher, wolverines, skunks, otter and lynx.

Cochrane mascot Chimo the Polar Bear.

The historic 1908 Cochrane Union Station has had a roof lift to accommodate a hotel and larger restaurant.

Routes for the Serious Canoeist

There are three challenging routes to the Moose River and then on to Moosonee. The return trip can be on the Big or Little Bear trains.

The Mattagami River covers 326 kilometres and ten to twelve days should suffice for the run. There are nine portages and help can be more than a day's travel away.

The Missinaibi River is also remote and its 320 kilometres take about nine days to complete, although it can take longer in late summer. There are up to ten portages, of which the longest is three kilometres.

The Abitibi River is also relatively remote and its 280 kilometre length should take ten to twelve days of paddling. Hydro dams have eased out some of the former rapids, but there are still five portages.

Tides on the River

Tides are caused by the gravitational pull of the moon and the sun and by the spinning or centrifugal force of the earth. The two daily cycles of high and low tides run fifty minutes later from one day to the next. Every two weeks at full and new moon the high tides or springs occur. A week later the neap or lower tides take place.

Tidal change in southern James Bay is about two metres, but tidal effect is greater than might be thought as the Moose River delta is so flat that sandbars and mud flats are exposed for a distance of several kilometres at low tide. The Moose River is tidal for about 35 kilometres, or as far as the North French River. The water levels and tide times can be changed by wind strength. Since the early days of the fur trade, people along the river had to regulate ship sailings by the tides. Today canoes crossing between the mainland and Moose Factory still add an extra mile to their trip at low tide, to avoid rocky shoals and sandbars.

Do-it-Yourself Weather Forecasting

People in places like the Hudson Bay Lowlands have always paid close attention to signs that fortell changes in the weather. Here are some; readers may wish to add observations of their own.

- A loon flying and calling—rain within 24 hours
- Birds flying high in the sky—windy weather within 24 hours
- Much grasshopper song and activity—hot and dry weather on the way
- Rain in the morning and overcast clouds moving in opposite direction to ground wind—clearing skies by noon
- Sundogs or partial rings around the sun—rain or unsettled weather
- Very warm days and later feathery clouds—thunder storm overnight
- Dew on the grass early in the morning—clear warm day

A Contribution from the Ontario Ministry of Natural Resources

The MNR has a fine interpretive centre on the Moose River not far north of the docks which is well worth a visit. They have pamphlets on wildlife and displays of birds and mammals. Some observations made by ministry personnel talk about the wider area covered by the district of the same name which extends beyond Moosonee:

- The Moosonee District covers twenty-two percent of the land mass of Ontario but has only enough people for a small town elsewhere.
- Hudson and James Bays are the province's only salt water coasts.
- One of the world's most extensive polar bear tagging programmes takes place to the north at the Polar Bear Provincial Park.
- Moosonee and Moose Factory make up the largest Cree community in Canada.
- The District has the largest number of golden eagle nesting sites in the province.
- The District has the world's most extensive muskeg and the third largest peat reserves.
- The District is the only place in Ontario where beluga whales, polar bears, walrus, and bearded and ringed seals are seen in the wild.

Of Interest to Naturalists

Among **wild flowers** are violets, some orchids, including the yellow ladyslipper and the ringed green, marsh marigold, rue

Lake Commanda, adjacent to Cochrane's railway station, is a pleasant picnic spot.

The addition of an extra storey to house a hotel gave new life to the historic Cochrane Union Station.

anemone, pipissewas, common vetch, clover, bunchberry, evening primrose, bluebells, Indian paintbrush, wood lily and nodding trillium.

Wild berries include strawberries, raspberries, red and black currants, chokecherries and high bush cranberries.

Rock hounds will find fossils up to 350 million years old. Look for trilobites, brachiopods, gastropods and crinoids. Onyx, once material for arrowheads, is found in black, brown, green and red.

Year-round **bird** residents are the Canada jay, black-capped and chestnut-backed chickadee, ruffled and spruce grouse, ptarmigan and ravens. Fine weather residents are Canada geese, along with blues, wavies and snows.

Summer visitors are the robins, fox, song and white-crowned sparrows, juncos, pine grosbeaks and warblers. Among the water birds are kingfishers and herring gulls. Some enthusiasts have suggested that fifty-eight birds frequent the area.

Among the **animals,** moose are conspicuous by their absence, although there are some in fringe areas. Caribou range as far south as Lake Kasagami. Local trappers take marten, beaver, muskrat, fox and otter. There are few black bears and wolves but weasels, mice, moles and rabbits are common.

Within a short distance of Moose Factory, **fish** taken include pickerel, pike, suckers, trout and white fish. Lake Kasagami is one of the best fishing spots.

A Few Words of Cree

Local telephone directories, advertisements and the newspaper give family names of Cree residents. Some are Scots names dating back to the early fur trading days. More common traditional names are those like Cheena, Quachegan, Whiskeychan, Cheechoo, Nakogie, Hookimow, Kooses and Chookomolin. James Evans, a Methodist missionary, developed the syllabics which enable written communication in Cree. The system is still used and taught in schools. The angular writing, somewhat like Gregg shorthand in appearance, is not difficult to learn. The Cree have also adapted English words to their own use. There are many dialects, usually characterized by the different endings of words. In this area alone there is Moose Cree, East Coast and West Coast versions of the language around James Bay. Try some of these words using the syllabarium as a pronounciation guide.

Hello *Watch-ee-ay*   How are You? *Taw-ne-tee-an?*
Fine or good *Ma-naw-shin*   It is a nice day *Mee-low-gee-she-gow*
Thank you *Mee-gwich*   Yes *Eh-eh*
Minister (church boss) *Em- weh- gum- ik*
Sunday (prayer day)   *a-yu-mih-o-kee-shi-kak*

One example of how the language has adapted to changing times came when it was necessary in the early thirties to describe a steam engine on the railway.

Scoo-tayo toban maiskano
fire   sleigh   path or trail

ONTARIO NORTHLAND

ONR logo with the distinctive tire tread symbolizing all its operations. These even have colour swatches!

Recipes and Medicines

Maryann Sams' *Wagunabuie* or Lichen Soup

Pick moss and wash well. Use water in which fish, fish eggs or meat has been boiled. Stir well while cooking. Add salt. Boil until tender. Put the fish or meat back into the water. Stir and serve hot.

Juliette Iserhoff's Bannock with Currants

Bannock is first-rate bread. This recipe calls for an oven but it can be made over an open fire.

Take 6 cups flour
1 cup lard
3 tablespoons baking powder
1 tablespoon salt
 2 cups currants
 3 or 4 cups water.

Mix the flour and lard by hand. Then add other ingredients. Add the water and make a dough. Place the dough in two 8-inch cake pans and bake in oven for 30-40 minutes. This makes 8-10 servings.

Maryann Sam's Pemmican

Pemmican is a great energy source for those travelling and working outdoors. Versions of this recipe have been used in the north for hundreds of years.

Use dried, powdered fish with lard or fat from bear, goose, caribou or moose. Pound the mixture and mix it like a batter. Some people mix in berries and sugar. Keep it frozen. In summer the same mixture may be made more like a dough as it will keep well. A piece the size of a date square is enough for a meal and goes well with a cup of tea.

And for various ailments try:

- boiled wild strawberry root mixed with sugar for diarrhea
- inside strips of spruce wood for burns
- warm spruce gum on a cloth for boils, cuts and sores
- muskrat or beaver fur laid over painful areas to remove pain.

Song of the Train

Some years ago the Polar Bear Express was the inspiration for a song produced on 45 rpm format. Here is a sample of the lyrics.

> Ride, ride the Polar Bear Express
> Toss all your troubles to the wind
> Ride, ride the Polar Bear Express
> It's God's country you're in.

Title is *The Polar Bear Express*. Alex Zanetis produced the disk for the Polar Bear label, care of Jack 0' Diamonds, Inc., Box 504, Nashville, Tennessee, U.S.A.

Original Temiskaming and Northern Ontario Railway steam engine #137 heads cars housing the local railway museum.

10

Finding Out More

CUSTOMARILY the reader looks for a bibliography to find out more about the subject of interest. In the case of the communities at the bottom of the Bay, there are many books, articles and pamphlets but most have only a fleeting concern with the area or are not readily available. Instead some works are offered with a brief commentary. Most are either available or found in public libraries and may be reliably taken as a good read.

Adult

Barnes, Michael. *Link with a Lonely Land*. Erin: Boston Mills/General, 1985

> This tells the story of the railway – first the Temiskaming and Northern Ontario Railway and later the Ontario Northland – largely through the people who made it a transportation success.

Barnes, Michael. *Policing Ontario-The OPP Today*. Erin: Boston Mills, 1991.

> The on-the-job story of the provincial police includes Moosonee and similar isolated areas.

Barnes, Michael. *Great Northern Characters*. Burnstown: GSPH, 1995.

> Twenty-five profiles of remarkable northerners including James Evans, inventor of the syllabics used by the Cree, Anglican Bishop of Moosonee Robert Renison, as well as two impostors who became "Indians" for widely differing reasons.

Kenyon, W.A., Turnbull, J.R. *The Battle for James Bay 1686*. Toronto, Macmillan, 1971.

> This is the only account in book form of some of the fights for supremacy between English and French fur trade interests.

Milberry, Larry. *Austin Airways: Canada's Oldest Airline*. Toronto: Canav, 1984.

> The adventures of early air service around James and Hudson Bays. The mantle of Austin Airways is now taken on by Air Creebec.

Juvenile

Barnes, Michael. *Message to Moosonee*. Cobalt: Highway, 1976.

> This short novel of four children who solve a mystery brings in familiar places at the end of the line.

Barnes, Michael. *Ontario*. Minneapolis: Lerner, 1995. (distributed in Canada by Nelson).

> This account of the province gives a good overview of Northern Ontario.

≫

The Freighter. Published at 50 cents, "carrying news to the James Bay coast." Purchase the paper at Moosonee or order through 500 Lamminen, Timmins, ON P4N 4R3, telephone (705) 268-4282.

This weekly newspaper is a great mirror of life at Moosonee and Moose Factory.

Acknowledgements

People make the north such an interesting place. Some of those who kindly assisted the author in research and travel were:

Wendy Kirk, editor of *The Freighter*, and her husband John, a most willing chauffeur;

Judy Cardoni, of the Ontario Northland's Public Affairs Department, and her assistant Glenn Fairey who provided information about the railway;

Anne-Marie Farrington of Air Creebec who paved the way north with both information and a flight on the busy Cree-owned line;

OPP officers Deb Bowerman and Don Daley who made the writer welcome on patrol. Police officers are always knowledgeable about the places where they work;

Members of the Mocreebec and Moose Band who were most helpful;

Two Bay Enterprizes owners Carol and Bishop Hennessy who provided transport and counsel, and their son, Martin, operator of the firm's tour arm, who was a cheerful guide.

Then there were all those who loaned photographs, as well as Cree photographer Paul McLeod, a good source of images of people and life at the bottom of the Bay.

Thanks to all the folks who live on the Moose River; they are a fine bunch, and their quality is like the old Hudson Bay Company standard for its customers, the best procurable!

About the Author

Michael Barnes is the author of *Great Northern Characters,* published by General Store Publishing House in 1995. He has written more than thirty books on northern Ontario, has several weekly newspaper columns and broadcasts on historical topics for the CBC.

In the mid sixties he was Supervising Principal of the schools then in operation on Moose Factory Island. Since that time he has kept in close touch with life at the bottom of the Bay.

He was appointed to the Order of Canada in 1995 for his body of writing on the north and makes his home in Haliburton, Ontario.

email: michaelbarnes53@hotmail.com

To order more copies of

Ride the **POLAR BEAR** *Express*

MICHAEL BARNES

Visiting MOOSONEE and MOOSE FACTORY

Contact:

GENERAL STORE PUBLISHING HOUSE

499 O'Brien Road, Box 415
Renfrew, Ontario Canada K7V 4A6
Telephone: 1-800-465-6072
Fax: (613) 432-7184
www.gsph.com

VISA and MASTERCARD accepted.